The Fortre

The Fortress Within

The Fortress Within is a rare gem in the modern self-help canon, unafraid to speak about virtue, fatherhood, financial stewardship, and spiritual warfare in the same breath. It's not merely a book; it's a compass for men (and families) who feel lost in a culture that rewards passivity and disconnection. David Fletcher has written something not just worth reading, but worth living by.

With raw honesty and grounded wisdom, Fletcher walks the reader through a tripartite framework: spiritual resilience, moral clarity, and financial discipline. His voice is fatherly, accessible, and sincere, inviting the reader to build not just a life, but a legacy.

Whether you are a young father, a man in search of meaning, or someone who wants to live a life of integrity and courage, this book will speak to you. It's a toolkit. A confession. A brotherly hand on the shoulder.

Read it slowly. Reflect deeply. Live it fully.

Contents

CERTA VIRILITER SVSTINE PATIENTER

[4]

The Fortress Within: Building a Spiritual, Moral, and Financial Legacy as a Catholic Man

Introduction: The War is Within

The greatest battle a man will ever fight is not on some distant battlefield or against a visible enemy, it is the battle within his own soul. Every day, countless men wake up already in the midst of a war they may barely perceive: a war between virtue and vice, faith and doubt, courage and fear. This internal struggle defines who we become. As the Catechism of the Catholic Church starkly observes, "the whole world...is in the power of the evil one", a dramatic situation that "makes man's life a battle". From the dawn of history, men have had to struggle to do what is right, and with God's grace achieve what the Catechism calls "inner integrity"

In other words, the war is real, and it is within. We live in an age of compromise and confusion. Society offers men comfort instead of character, relativism instead of truth, indulgence instead of discipline. The modern world praises wealth, pleasure, and power, yet so often it leaves men feeling spiritually empty and morally adrift. You might be a young man bombarded by temptations and mixed messages about what it means to be "successful." You might be a husband and father fighting to protect your family from corrosive cultural influences. You might simply be a man who wants to do right but finds himself falling short in a world that makes it so easy to do wrong. In all these cases, the real war, the most consequential conflict, is fought not in the news headlines or on social media, but in the quiet recesses of your heart, where decisions of eternal importance are made. The Fortress Within is about winning that war. It is about building an unshakable stronghold of faith, virtue, and discipline deep in your soul, a "fortress" that no temptation or trial can easily topple. This fortress is not made of stone and steel, but of spiritual strength, moral clarity, and wise stewardship of the gifts God has given you. The walls of this inner citadel are constructed from your daily habits and choices; its foundation is Jesus Christ, the solid rock upon which a meaningful life is built (cf. Matthew 7:24-25). With God's help, you can become a man of God who stands firm no matter how fierce the cultural storms rage outside. This guide is structured into four parts, each addressing a pillar of that inner fortress. In Part I: Spiritual Strength – Becoming a Man of God, we will lay the spiritual foundation: developing a genuine relationship with God through prayer, the sacraments, and trust in divine grace. In Part II: Moral Clarity – Living with Integrity in a Compromised World, we will raise the walls of virtue: learning to live honestly, purely, and courageously according to Catholic moral teaching despite the world's compromises. In Part III: Financial Discipline – Building a Legacy, Not Just Wealth, we will examine how to master our financial life with wisdom and generosity, so that money serves rather than enslaves, and our prosperity becomes a legacy of good. Finally, in Part IV: Integration – Living the Legacy Daily, we will bring it all together, crafting a daily way of life that consistently reflects our faith and values, and ensuring we persevere with support from our brothers in Christ. Each part contains chapters that delve deep, these are not checklists or platitudes, but full explorations with real stories, concrete teachings, and practical exercises. You will find narrative examples drawn from lived experience, teachings rooted in Sacred Scripture and Catholic tradition, personal reflection prompts to challenge and illumine your own journey, and clear action steps to help you put principles into practice. Think of it as a training manual for the soul. Just as an army trains rigorously before battle, we too must train our hearts and minds for the spiritual combat we face daily.

As you read, remember that building this fortress within is a gradual process, brick by brick, day by day. There will be setbacks and failures; every warrior stumbles. But do not be discouraged. God's mercy is always ready to forgive, His strength always available to those who ask. No man builds a great legacy overnight. Rather, it is in the daily choices, the hidden sacrifices, and the persevering prayer that you will forge your character. By the end of this book, you will have a blueprint for your own spiritual fortification: a plan to become the man God created you to be, for His glory and the good of those you love. The world today desperately needs men of principle and prayer, men who are unafraid to love God wholeheartedly, to live with integrity, and to lead their families with wisdom. Such men become like lighted watchtowers in a dark landscape, guiding others to safety and truth. This is your calling. It's time to step onto the battlefield with confidence in Christ. It's time to build the fortress within.

Part I: Spiritual Strength – Becoming a Man of God

"I can do all things through Him who strengthens me." (Philippians 4:13)

Chapter 1: A Son of God in the King's Service

The Fortress Within

The Fortress Within

Narrative: I still remember the morning I realized I had been fighting the wrong battles. In my early twenties, I thought I had life figured out. I lived for the moment, chasing pleasure, fuelled by drink, drugs, and the thrill of indulgence. I wore my atheism like Armor, confident that God was a crutch for the weak and that I was in control of my destiny. I filled my time with noise: late nights, loud music, shallow relationships, and the next temporary high. If you had asked me then, I would've told you I was thriving, that I had found freedom. But under the surface, I was restless. Even in the middle of the party, something felt hollow. What shook me wasn't a tragedy, but a question. As I dove deeper into science, the very thing I once thought disproved faith, I started to see something different. The structure of the universe, the fine-tuning of nature, the precision of life itself... it didn't scream randomness. It whispered design. And design demands a Designer. That line of thought became the crack in the foundation of my worldview. Slowly, almost reluctantly, I began to entertain the idea that maybe, just maybe, I didn't know everything. Maybe the story was bigger than me. Around this time quite a long relationship ended, and a new one began. I found myself sitting alone in the back of a quiet church. I hadn't gone there looking for God. But something, or Someone, had drawn me in. In the silence of that sanctuary, I confronted the one question I had been avoiding: What am I really living for? It was then that something changed. Not a dramatic vision, not a lightning bolt, just a quiet but undeniable truth settling into my heart: I am a son of God, created to know Him, love Him, and serve Him. All my life, I had dismissed the idea of God as wishful thinking. But now I knew, not with arrogance, but with conviction, that I had been wrong. Being a man isn't about proving strength or mastering pleasure. It's about knowing who you belong to. And I belonged to a Father who had been patiently waiting for me all along.

Called to Be Sons of the King: Every Catholic man has this identity at the core of his being: son of the Heavenly Father. We are not spiritual orphans fending for ourselves in a meaningless universe. We have a Father who loved us into existence and a King who died to save us. By baptism, we were claimed by God and enlisted in the service of Christ the King. This is why the Church can boldly say that each of us is called to nothing less than holiness. In fact, "Every Catholic man is called to give himself fully to Jesus Christ and His Catholic Church"

God doesn't merely want us to be 'nice guy' or 'good enough' people, he calls us to be saints, to share in His divine life and to reflect His goodness in the world. As one Catholic author put it, "There are no nice people or good people in Heaven, only Saints. Most men have not made a commitment to strive for Sainthood. Men are stuck in mediocrity and need to raise the bar higher; there is no higher bar than Sainthood."

This can sound intimidating, but it's actually the most exciting adventure possible. It means your life has a noble purpose: to become the man God intended you to be, a man of virtue bound for heaven. The Spiritual Battlefield: However, discovering our identity as sons of God also opens our eyes to the battle that rages around and within us. If we truly belong to Christ, we become enemy number one for the devil. Make no mistake, Satan is real, hell is real, and sin is real.

Behind the troubles of the world lurks an evil one who "prowls around like a roaring lion, seeking someone to devour" (1 Peter 5:8). Our secular culture often ignores or even mocks the idea of the devil, but a man of God recognizes that he faces not only his own weaknesses but also a real spiritual opponent. The good news is that Jesus Christ has already conquered sin and death; our task is to live in His victory. But it will involve fighting, first and foremost, fighting the temptations and vices that wage war in our own hearts (cf. James 4:1). When you were confirmed, you were sealed with the Holy Spirit and strengthened as a soldier of Christ. You were given armour and weapons, spiritually speaking, to stand against evil. The battle is not easy, but you are not alone in it. God's grace is your supply line, and the communion of saints, countless holy men who have gone before you, stands as your comrades and guides. Consider the example of Saint Augustine. As a young man, Augustine was brilliant but wayward; he chased pleasures and worldly knowledge, ignoring his devout mother Monica's pleas to turn to God. He later wrote in his Confessions about how empty he felt after indulging every lust and ambition. His heart was restless. Only when he finally surrendered to God, acknowledging himself as a lost son returning to the Father, did Augustine find the peace and strength he longed for. He became one of the Church's greatest saints and thinkers, proving that no matter how far off-track we might go, our Father's call remains: "Come back to Me with all your heart" (cf. Joel 2:12). Augustine discovered that being a man of God meant humbly accepting that he needed God. In his famous words to the Lord, "You have made us for Yourself, and our hearts are restless until they rest in You." Embracing Your High Calling: To be a son of God in the King's service means two key things: relationship and mission. First, relationship: God invites you into an intimate Father-son relationship with Him. This is not merely a metaphor; it's a spiritual reality. Through prayer and sacrament (which we'll explore in the next chapter), you have access to your Father's heart. You can know Him, speak with Him, receive His wisdom and love. Jesus taught us to pray "Our Father", showing that we approach God as beloved children, not as slaves of a distant master. Knowing you are a son gives you confidence and identity. Even when you fail or sin, you can repent and return like the prodigal son, knowing your Father eagerly awaits your return (Luke 15:20-24). Second, mission: as a son of God, you are also a servant of His kingdom. Every king's son in history had duties to represent the crown; how much more do we, sons of the eternal King, have the duty to represent Christ in the world? This means living in such a way that others see something of God's goodness through us. It means bearing witness to the truth and love of Christ in our daily interactions. It also means actively working to advance God's kingdom, by sharing our faith, defending the weak, doing our work honestly and well, raising godly families, and serving those in need. If this sounds like a lot, remember that God never asks us to do it alone or overnight. He promises, "I am with you always" (Matthew 28:20) and gives us the strength for every task He calls us to. As Saint Paul wrote, "We are ambassadors for Christ" (2 Corinthians 5:20). Embracing your sonship will naturally lead you to embrace being an ambassador of the King in your corner of the world. In practical terms, start by reaffirming in your mind and heart who you really are. You are not defined by your pay check, your status, or your sins, you are defined by the Father who created you and the Son who redeemed you. When you wake up each morning, remind yourself: I am a son of God, called to be a saint. This affirmation isn't wishful thinking; it's the truth. We have to internalize that truth, because the world will try to make us forget it at every turn. Our consumer culture will try to label you as a "customer" who exists to buy things. Corporate life might treat you as a "resource" or a cog in a machine. Sadly, some toxic social environments might reduce men to stereotypes or tell you that you're "just an animal" ruled by passions. Reject those lies. You are a child of God, endowed with a soul, reason, and a conscience. You carry the imprint of your Father in heaven.

Reflection: Take a moment to reflect on your own sense of identity. Do you truly see yourself as God's beloved son? Where do you derive your self-worth, from your relationship with God, or from the opinions of others and worldly success? How might your life choices change if you more fully embraced the truth that you were made for holiness and greatness in God's eyes? Action Steps:

Personal Mission Statement: Write down a simple statement of life purpose that reflects your identity as a Catholic man. For example: "I am a son of God, called to know, love, and serve Him. My mission is to become a saint and lead others to heaven, especially my family." Place this somewhere you will see it daily.

Litany of Saints: Choose a patron saint (or two) who inspires you as a model of manhood (e.g., Saint Joseph for fatherly strength, Saint Francis for humility, Saint Augustine for conversion). Read a short biography or quote from them. Ask for their intercession in prayer. Remember that the saints are your spiritual brothers, cheering you on.

Daily Surrender: Each morning this week, upon waking, pray a simple prayer of surrender to God, such as: "Lord, I am Your son. I offer You this day and all I do. Help me to serve You faithfully." This reinforces who you are living for each day.

Chapter 2: Fuel for the Soul – Prayer and Sacraments

The Fortress Within

Narrative: Imagine a warrior who never sharpens his sword or a marathon runner who never eats healthy food. No matter how strong or determined they might be, eventually they will falter because they've neglected the very things that give them strength. Early in my spiritual journey, I experienced a similar reality. After that awakening in the church where I realized my identity as a son of God, I felt inspired, for a while. But inspiration alone wasn't enough. In the weeks that followed, I struggled to maintain my resolve. I would wake up intending to live as a man of faith, but by midday I'd be swept up in work stress and distractions. I often skipped praying because I "didn't have time." Sunday Mass sometimes felt dry and obligatory, so I would tune out or find excuses to miss when life got busy. Slowly, that initial fire I felt began to dim. I realized that if I didn't fuel my soul regularly, my spiritual strength would wither. Like a phone that needs recharging or a car that needs gas, my heart needed daily prayer and frequent grace from the sacraments to run well. This chapter is about discovering those sources of supernatural strength and making them a non-negotiable part of your life. The Power of Daily Prayer: Prayer is to the soul what oxygen is to the body. It is our direct line of communication with God, the lifeline of our identity and mission. Yet, many men struggle with prayer, finding time for it, knowing how to do it, or believing it truly matters. Perhaps you've felt awkward trying to pray, or you've gone through the motions of rote prayers without feeling much. That's okay. The key is to start where you are and keep at it, because prayer will

[20]

transform you over time. Scripture tells us to "pray without ceasing" (1 Thessalonians 5:17), which underscores how central prayer is meant to be in a Christian's life. If you want to be a man of God, daily prayer is non-negotiable. It's the daily meeting with your Commanding Officer, the quiet briefing where you receive your orders, your encouragement, and your refreshment. How can you begin? If you don't already have a habit of prayer, start simple. Set aside just 10-15 minutes every morning to be alone with God. Find a quiet spot (maybe a favourite chair or a corner of your room). You can start by reading a short passage from Scripture, perhaps one of the Gospels or the Psalms, and then talk to God about it. Speak to Him as a Father and friend: thank Him for a new day, ask Him for guidance and protection, share what's on your heart. Then make sure to spend a couple of minutes in silence, listening. At first, your mind will wander, that's normal. Gently bring it back. Over time, you'll find this morning prayer time becomes a source of peace and clarity for your whole day. Remember, the goal of prayer is not to have a dramatic experience every time, but to build a relationship. Just like any friendship, consistency matters more than feelings in the moment. One practical tip: incorporate prayer into existing routines. For example, if you drive to work, turn off the radio for part of the commute and speak to God. If you exercise, say a decade of the Rosary during a cool-down walk. Pray with Scripture by using resources like the daily Mass readings or a devotional app. The exact method isn't as important as the commitment to show up before God each day. You might be surprised how quickly 15 minutes can pass once you get going. In fact, many men who start with 15 minutes eventually hunger for more as they taste the goodness of time with God. Encountering God in the Mass: If prayer is our lifeline, the Holy Mass is like entering the throne room of the King. It is the "source and summit" of our Catholic faith. Yet, surveys and personal testimonies show that a large number of Catholic men struggle to connect with the Mass. Perhaps you've heard men say (or thought yourself), "Mass is boring; I don't get anything out of it." The truth is that if Mass feels boring, it's often because we don't understand what's truly happening there. At every Mass, the veil between heaven and earth is torn open: we are present at the foot of the Cross, witnessing Jesus Christ's sacrifice made present again (in an unbloody manner) on the altar

Bread and wine are transformed into the Body and Blood of Christ, yes, the same Jesus who died and rose again. And then we are invited to receive Him in Holy Communion, uniting us with God in the most intimate way. This is anything but boring! It's earth-shattering. The Son of God comes to nourish you with His very self. If we approach Mass with faith and preparation, it becomes a wellspring of strength. Make it a point to attend Mass every Sunday without fail, it's not only an obligation, but a privilege. Plan your weekend around Mass, not the other way around. If Sunday morning is chaotic for your family, try a vigil Mass on Saturday or a different time that allows for a more prayerful approach. Before Mass, take a few moments to read the readings (many apps and websites provide the daily Mass readings). That way, when you hear them proclaimed, you're already tuned in. During the Mass, remember you are at Calvary: when the priest lifts up the Host and the Chalice, in your heart say, "My Lord and my God!" recognizing Jesus present. When you receive Communion, realize that you are a living tabernacle, Jesus is within you. Speak to Him in those precious minutes after Communion; thank Him and tell Him what you need. Beyond Sunday, consider going to Mass one extra time during the week or visiting Jesus in Eucharistic Adoration. Even 30 minutes in Adoration, simply sitting or kneeling in the presence of the Eucharist, can recharge your soul in remarkable ways.

Many saints and holy men testify that all the troubles and decisions of life look different when placed before Jesus in the Blessed Sacrament. If you feel burdened or confused, bring it to Him there. This might mean giving up a lunch break or getting up earlier, but the peace you receive will more than repay the effort. The Grace of Confession: Alongside the Eucharist, the Sacrament of Reconciliation (Confession) is a powerhouse for spiritual growth. It's also one many men tend to avoid or put off. Perhaps you haven't gone to Confession in years and the thought of telling your sins to a priest makes you break out in a sweat. Or maybe you go occasionally but only out of duty and feel no different after. Let's reframe Confession: it is not a humiliating checklist, but an encounter with the mercy of Jesus that liberates and heals you. Picture a soldier stumbling under heavy gear and wounds; Confession is where the Divine Physician takes that weight off your back and tends to your wounds. Christ instituted this sacrament because He knows we need to hear the words "You are forgiven" spoken to us (see John 20:22-23). There's immense psychological and spiritual relief in an honest confession. Make it a habit to go to Confession regularly, once a month is a good target, or more often if you're struggling with serious sin. Don't wait until you're perfect; go because you're not perfect. When you confess your sins sincerely and hear the priest's absolution, you receive grace that strengthens you against those sins in the future. Men who commit to frequent Confession often find that sins which used to dominate them (like habitual lying, outbursts of anger, or sexual sins) begin to lose their grip. It's not magic; it's grace reorienting your heart and strengthening your will. Keep in mind that priests have heard it all, your sins won't shock them. They are there to help you, not to judge you. If you're nervous, tell the priest it's been a while; he will gently guide you. Remember, God never tires of forgiving; it is we who tire of asking. So ask, and receive the freedom of a clean soul. Other Spiritual Fuel: Scripture and Devotion: In addition to the sacraments and personal prayer, two other "fuels" deserve special mention: Scripture and devotional practices. The Bible is not just an old book of stories; it is the living Word of God and a spiritual sword (Ephesians 6:17) for battle.

The Fortress Within

When you read the Word of God, you invite the Holy Spirit to speak truth into your life. Try to spend at least a few minutes a day reading Scripture. You could read the Gospel of the day, or slowly work through one of the Gospels or epistles, or use a Bible-in-a-year plan. Don't worry about understanding everything at once. Listen for one thought or verse that strikes you and carry it in your mind. Over time, the Scriptures will begin to echo in your thoughts, guiding and consoling you in various situations. Devotional practices, like praying the Rosary, are another tried-and-true way to draw closer to God. The Rosary in particular has been called "the weapon for these times" by saints and popes. It might seem repetitive, but in its gentle rhythm of prayers and mysteries, the Rosary leads us to meditate on the life of Christ with the guidance of His mother, Mary. Carrying a Rosary with you and praying it regularly (even a decade at a time) is an act of loyalty and faith. Many of the greatest saints and even battle-hardened soldiers prayed the Rosary; it steeled them with courage and kept their focus on Jesus. Our Lady is a powerful intercessor, when you ask her to pray for you, she brings your needs straight to her Son. Especially if you struggle with purity or with anxiety, the Rosary is a balm and a shield. Give it a chance; you might be surprised at the inner calm and strength that develop after making the Rosary a regular habit. Lastly, develop a relationship with your patron saints and guardian angel. These heavenly allies are part of your support team. If you were confirmed, you likely chose a patron saint, learn more about him (or her) and pray for their intercession. The Communion of Saints means we are never alone; those who have gone before us are cheering us on and helping us with their prayers. Your guardian angel, assigned to you by God, is also real and active, ask for their guidance and protection, especially in moments of temptation or danger. It might feel strange at first to pray to someone you can't see, but remember that in God's design, we are part of a family that spans heaven and earth. Reflection: Consider your spiritual "fuel gauge." Are you running on fumes? Do you rush through days and weeks with little prayer, irregular Mass attendance, or unconfessed sins weighing you down? How do you currently experience Mass and prayer, are they sources of strength or just duties? Be honest. God invites you to a deeper experience of His grace. What barriers (schedule, laziness, doubt) hold you back from regular prayer or sacraments, and how could you begin to overcome them? Action Steps:

Daily Prayer Commitment: If you don't pray daily, start with 10 minutes each morning this coming week. Protect this time, treat it as an important meeting. Use a timer if needed. Read a short Scripture passage and talk to God about your day. If you already pray daily, consider extending your time or adding a second prayer moment (like 10 minutes at night to review your day and thank God).

Mass and Adoration: Attend one weekday Mass or an hour of Eucharistic Adoration in the next two weeks (in addition to Sunday). Put it on your calendar. Bring a concern or decision you're facing and lay it before Jesus in the Eucharist. Observe the difference in your peace of mind afterward.

Confession Plan: Schedule your next Confession right now. Mark a date on your calendar (ideally within the next month). Before going, do an examination of conscience (using the Ten Commandments or a guide from a Catholic app/parish pamphlet). After confession, note how you feel, and consider making this a monthly routine so that grace can continually renew you.

Scripture & Rosary: Pick one: either commit to reading Scripture for at least 5 minutes a day (perhaps with your morning coffee or before bed), or start praying the Rosary (even a decade daily to begin). For Scripture, a good starting point is one of the Gospels (Mark is the shortest). For the Rosary, carry one in your pocket and use your commute or a walk to pray. Track your practice for one week and note any changes in your perspective.

Chapter 3: Armoured by Faith – Virtue and Spiritual Warfare

The Fortress Within

The Fortress Within

Narrative: Every man, no matter how devout, has felt the pull of temptation. For me, one of the early wake-up calls in my journey came through something I never expected would be a battlefield: my own temper. It had been a long two days, back-to-back meetings, forced smiles, endless pitches. The sales convention had drained me more than I realized. Delayed travel only added to the exhaustion. By the time I walked through the front door that evening, I was running on fumes, mentally fried, emotionally frayed. My wife, just trying to reconnect after the time apart, asked me how it went. A simple, innocent question. But instead of gratitude or warmth, what came out of me was sharp, biting frustration. I snapped. Words I didn't mean. Tone I would never have chosen. The moment they left my mouth, I saw it, the look on her face. Hurt. Stunned. Silent. That image haunted me all night. It pierced deeper than any business failure or missed opportunity ever could. That night, after apologizing, I knelt and prayed like a man desperate for help. I saw clearly that there was a battle raging in me: my pride and anger versus the patience and love God was calling me to. It felt like war, because it was. Not a war of guns and swords, but an internal battle for my soul and my character. I knew then that if I wanted to be a man of God, I had to learn how to fight spiritually. I needed to put on some armour and take up some weapons. The Reality of Spiritual Warfare: We touched already on the idea that we have an enemy, the devil, who seeks our downfall. But spiritual warfare isn't only about external demonic attacks; it's also about battling our own sinful inclinations, which Scripture often calls the "flesh" (our fallen human nature). Saint Peter admonishes us: "Discipline yourselves, keep alert. Like a roaring lion your adversary the devil prowls around, looking for someone to devour. Resist him, firm in your faith" (1 Peter 5:8-9). This tells us two crucial things: we must stay alert (vigilant), and our faith is the key to resistance. The good news is that God has given us all we need to fight and win. Ephesians 6:11-18 describes the armour of God: the belt of truth, breastplate of righteousness, shoes of readiness for the Gospel of peace, shield of faith, helmet of salvation, and sword of the Spirit (the word of God). These are images for virtues and spiritual resources that protect us from the enemy's attacks. For example, living truthfully and with integrity (belt of truth) protects us from Satan's lies and deception. Pursuing righteousness and holiness (breastplate) guards our heart from the corrosion of sin. Faith acts as a shield that can "extinguish all the flaming arrows of the evil one" (Eph 6:16), meaning the doubts, temptations, and discouragements the devil hurls at us. Think of a common temptation, say the lure of pornography or any lustful thought. If you walk unarmed into that temptation, relying on sheer willpower at the moment of crisis, you're likely to fall. But if you approach the battlefield armoured—knowing ahead of time this is a weakness, praying for strength, avoiding triggers (like installing a filter on your devices or not being alone idly late at night), and holding onto the shield of faith (trusting that God's plan for sexuality is better than the cheap lure of lust)—then you have a fighting chance. Add to that the sword of the Spirit, which can be as simple as recalling a Scripture verse in the moment of temptation (for instance, quoting Job 31:1: "I have made a covenant with my eyes; how then could I gaze at a virgin?" as a personal pledge to purity), and you begin to push the enemy back. Jesus Himself used Scripture as a sword when tempted by Satan in the desert (Matthew 4:1-11), responding to lies with God's Word. We should do the same. Building Virtue, Battling Vice: At the heart of spiritual warfare is the struggle between virtue and vice. Virtues are holy habits that make us more like Christ; vices are sinful habits that enslave us and make us easy targets for the enemy. To win the war within, we must actively cultivate virtue. The ancient philosophers and the Church speak of four cardinal virtues: Prudence (wise decision-making), Justice (giving others their due, including God), Fortitude (courage and endurance in doing good), and Temperance (self-control and moderation). Added to these are the three theological virtues given by God: Faith, Hope, and Charity (love). When you consistently practice virtues, you are essentially training your soul's "muscles" to act rightly with ease. This doesn't mean you become sinless, but you become stronger at resisting sin and doing good almost by second nature. Conversely, if you give in to a vice repeatedly, be it laziness, lust, anger, greed, you're training yourself in the wrong direction, making it harder to break free. It's like carving a negative groove in your character. But no vice is beyond God's grace to overcome. With patience, prayer, and perseverance, you can unlearn habits of sin and replace them with habits of virtue. An important strategy in spiritual combat is to identify your primary weak points. In traditional Catholic spirituality, this is sometimes called your "predominant fault" the vice that you struggle with most. For one man it might be pride (manifesting as arrogance or unwillingness to admit wrong), for another it might be lust, for another sloth (apathy and procrastination), for another greed or ambition at the expense of others. Once you name the enemy, you can craft a battle plan. If pride is your issue, deliberately practice humility: seek advice, apologize when wrong, do hidden acts of service. If anger (like mine) is your issue, practice meekness and patience: train yourself to pause and pray when provoked, perhaps saying internally "Jesus, meek and humble of heart, make my heart like Yours." If laziness is the problem, practice diligence: set a strict schedule for yourself and hold to it, even in small things like waking up on time and making your bed (little disciplines spill over into bigger ones). Whatever the vice, there is a corresponding virtue to cultivate. Over time, strengthening virtue is like reinforcing the walls of your fortress; the temptations might still batter at you, but they find no easy way in. Weapons of Self-Denial: While prayer and sacraments are primary, another classic weapon in spiritual warfare is self-denial or fasting. This may sound unpleasant, we naturally shy away from discomfort—but it's a powerful training method. When you deliberately deny yourself some legitimate pleasure or endure discomfort for the sake of discipline (offering it to God), you build spiritual toughness. Think of it as weightlifting for the will. For example, the Church traditionally asks us to abstain from meat on Fridays or do some form of penance to unite with Christ's sacrifice. You might also try occasionally fasting from a meal, or giving up social media for a day, or taking cold showers as a sacrifice. These practices aren't meant to punish us; they free us. They break the hold that our appetites have over us and tune our hearts to rely more on God's grace. If you can say no to yourself in small things, you'll find it easier to say no to sin in big things. And every time you feel that pinch of self-denial and still choose to endure it, you mimic Christ's own self-control and strengthen the virtue of temperance. Remember Your Training and Allies: In the thick of battle, a soldier relies on his training and trusts his comrades. In spiritual warfare, your "training" is your formation in the faith—Scripture, the wisdom of the Church, the sacraments—everything that shapes your conscience and resolve. Don't neglect ongoing formation: reading good spiritual books, attending retreats or men's conferences, or even regularly reading Scripture and catechism. This keeps your mind sharp and your strategy clear. Your comrades are your fellow believers and the saints. We'll talk more about brotherhood in a later chapter, but even now, remember that you don't have to fight alone. Have a friend you can call or text when you're feeling particularly tempted, someone who can pray for you in that moment. Sometimes just exposing the temptation to the light by telling a trusted brother can break the spell it has. And never underestimate the help of the saints and angels: calling on St. Michael the Archangel with the famous prayer ("defend us in battle, be our protection against the wickedness and snares of the devil") or invoking your guardian angel, can bring real assistance in moments of trial. Hope in God's Grace: Lastly, while we speak of battle and warfare, remember that the Christian attitude is not one of grim despair or constant fear. It is one of hope and confidence in God. Yes, life is a battle, but we know Christ is victorious and He empowers us to share in that victory. You may have some spiritual scars from past defeats, we all do. Do not let them define you or paralyze you. Instead, let them teach you where you need to fortify your defences. If you fell into a particular sin, don't simply resolve "I won't do that again." Ask why you fell. Were you tired, lonely, under stress? Did you neglect prayer? Identify the breach in the wall, and rebuild it stronger with God's help. Inner integrity, as the Catechism noted, is achieved "at great cost to oneself and aided by God's grace". It's okay that it costs effort, that effort, empowered by grace, is what makes you grow. When you resist temptation, even if your hands are shaking, you grow in spiritual muscle. When you fail but get up, go to Confession, and keep trying, you deal a blow to the devil's intentions, because he wants you to stay down. Remember Proverbs 24:16: "Though the righteous fall seven times, they rise again." Be that righteous man who rises again, fortified by God's mercy. Reflection: Take an inventory of your personal spiritual battles. What are the top one or two vices or temptations that consistently challenge you? How have you been handling them up until now? Have you been mostly reacting in the moment, or do you have a proactive strategy to combat them? Reflect on what "armour" you might be lacking, perhaps knowledge of the faith, consistency in prayer (shield of faith), or self-control (breastplate of righteousness). How could you better "arm" yourself for these battles with God's help? Action Steps:

Identify Your Predominant Weakness: Write down the chief struggle (or two) that you face (e.g., "Impatience with my family" or "Habitual procrastination" or "Pornography use"). Next to it, write a corresponding virtue to cultivate (e.g., patience, diligence, chastity). This week, research one practical way to work on that virtue (for example, patience could be practiced by deliberately letting someone else go first or by breathing deeply and counting to ten when provoked). Implement that practice daily.

Ephesians 6 Check: Read Ephesians 6:10-18 (the armour of God passage) in your Bible. List the six pieces of armour and honestly assess which you tend to neglect. For instance, do you engage with Scripture (sword of Spirit) regularly? Is your "helmet" of salvation secure meaning, do you remind yourself of your salvation and live with the hope of heaven? Choose one piece of armour to "put on" with extra attention each morning. For example, physically pray, "Lord, gird me with the belt of truth today" and resolve to speak and live truthfully that day.

Small Fast: Pick one day in the next week to practice a small fast or act of self-denial as spiritual training. It could be skipping lunch and offering up your hunger to God, or abstaining from sweets or coffee that day, or turning off all entertainment for 24 hours. When you feel the pinch, say a short prayer like, "Lord, this is for love of You. Strengthen me in the bigger battles." Observe how this act of discipline affects your ability to say no to yourself.

Fortify with Scripture and Prayer: Memorize one Scripture verse that directly counters a frequent temptation you face. For example, if you battle lust, memorize 1 Corinthians 6:19-20 ("Your body is a temple of the Holy Spirit..."). If anger, James 1:19 ("Be quick to hear, slow to speak, slow to anger"). Quote it when tempted. Additionally, consider adopting the St. Michael Prayer or another brief prayer to recite when you sense spiritual attack. This conditions you to turn to God immediately in the fight.

Part II: Moral Clarity – Living with Integrity in a Compromised World

"Do not be conformed to this world, but be transformed by the renewal of your mind, that you may discern what is the will of God, what is good and acceptable and perfect." (Romans 12:2)

Chapter 4: True North – Forming Your Conscience in Truth

The Fortress Within

The Fortress Within

Narrative: Mark was a top performer at his company, proud of his reputation for closing deals. One afternoon, his boss came to him with a request that made Mark's stomach drop: "We need to secure this contract. Just tell the client we can deliver by Q3, even though we both know it'll be Q4. We'll fix it later." In that moment, Mark felt a battle between his ambition and his integrity. A little voice inside, his conscience, whispered that lying to the client was wrong, but a louder voice of fear argued, "Everyone exaggerates in sales; if I don't do it, I might lose the account or my boss's trust." Mark excused himself to the restroom, looking in the mirror at a man uncertain of what to do. He remembered a lesson from a men's retreat he'd attended: never violate your conscience; it's your inner compass given by God. Taking a breath, he returned and respectfully told his boss, "I'm not comfortable making that promise. It wouldn't be true." The boss frowned, but Mark stood firm. It was a risk, but that day Mark realized that living with moral clarity often requires courage to stand by the truth, even when it costs. What is Conscience? Conscience is often described as the voice of God within us, guiding us to discern right from wrong. The Catechism teaches that conscience is a judgment of reason by which we recognize the moral quality of a concrete act (cf. CCC 1778). In simple terms, it's like an inner compass pointing to our "true north," which is the good and the true. But a compass only works correctly if it's calibrated. An improperly formed conscience can lead us astray, we might feel okay about doing something wrong, or feel guilty about something that's not actually wrong. Therefore, forming our conscience correctly is crucial. For a Catholic man, that means educating ourselves in God's truth as revealed in Scripture and taught by the Church. We don't invent right and wrong for ourselves; we discover moral truth through the light of reason and revelation. Jesus said, "You will know the truth, and the truth will make you free" (John 8:32). Moral truth isn't a cage to restrict us; it's a path to freedom and authentic love. In today's world, many say, "follow your heart" or "do what feels right." While intentions there might be good, encouraging authenticity, on its own this advice can be a trap. Our feelings can mislead us. A person could "feel" justified in holding a grudge or cheating if they've convinced themselves it's okay due to circumstances. That's why we need an objective standard: God's law, which is written on the human heart (Romans 2:15) but can be obscured by sin and society. To form your conscience, immerse yourself in those objective standards. The Ten Commandments, the teachings of Jesus (like the Beatitudes and the Sermon on the Mount), and the moral catechesis of the Church (found in the Catechism) are like detailed maps for the journey. They help align your inner compass with true north. For example, the world might say "It's okay to sleep with someone you love, even if you're not married; everyone does it," but Christ and the Church gently correct: sexual intimacy is a sacred gift for marriage (this will be discussed more in the next chapter). We might be tempted to think "a little white lie is fine if it helps avoid conflict," but Scripture says, "Speak the truth in love" (Ephesians 4:15). By regularly reading and reflecting on such teachings, we calibrate our conscience, so that gut feeling of right/wrong increasingly aligns with God's will. Integrity in a Compromised World: We live in a culture where moral lines are often blurred. What was once universally acknowledged as wrong might now be called acceptable or even virtuous under certain slogans. For instance, dishonesty is sometimes rebranded as "marketing" or "spin." Sexual immorality is labelled "personal freedom." Greed is praised as "success." In this environment, a Catholic man seeking moral clarity must be prepared to swim against the tide. "Do not be conformed to this world," St. Paul warns, "but be transformed by the renewal of your mind" (Romans 12:2). This renewal of mind is essentially forming and following a conscience rooted in truth rather than the latest popular opinion. There may be times when your values will conflict with what's normal at work or among friends. Perhaps everyone in the office cuts out early and falsifies their time sheet, or buddies pressure you to join in some unethical prank or outing. Integrity means doing the right thing even if no one else is, because you answer ultimately to God. It means your interior convictions and exterior actions match up, you are the same person alone as you are in public. It's helpful to remember that moral truth is not arbitrary. God's commandments are not random rules; they are instructions from the Designer about how we function best. Think of the manufacturer's manual for a machine, follow those guidelines, and the machine runs smoothly; violate them, and you cause damage. Similarly, living in line with God's moral law leads to human flourishing (even if it involves sacrifice), whereas living against it leads to harm (spiritually and often emotionally and physically too). For example, honesty builds trust and a clear conscience; dishonesty leads to stress, fractured relationships, and a divided self. Sexual purity leads to respect and true intimacy in God's time; sexual vice leads to broken hearts, insecurity, and using people as objects. Seeing the good fruits of virtue and the bad fruits of sin can reinforce our commitment to moral clarity. Beware Rationalizations: One of the biggest threats to moral clarity is rationalization, essentially lying to ourselves to justify something we know (deep down) is wrong. We all do it at times. We use softer words for our sins: "It's just a little porn, not hurting anyone," or "I'm not gossiping, I'm just sharing concerns," or "Everybody at work lies about their sales numbers, it's just how business is done." These are rationalizations, and they erode our integrity. As one commentator put it, moral clarity requires recognizing rationalization as the falsehood it is. To counter this, cultivate a habit of brutal honesty with yourself. When in doubt, ask: Am I telling myself the truth, or what I want to hear? If you find yourself bending the truth, even in your own mind, take it as a warning sign. It might help to speak with a good friend or mentor about the issue; saying it out loud can reveal if you're just making excuses. We should

[44]

prefer the ugly truth that leads to repentance than a pretty lie that lets us continue wrong. Remember King David, who rationalized his adultery with Bathsheba until the prophet Nathan confronted him with the truth (2 Samuel 12). David's greatness was not in being sinless, but in his willingness to repent once he faced the truth. Practical Steps to Moral Clarity: To maintain a clear moral compass, regular self-examination is key. Each day, perhaps at night, do a quick review of your actions and attitudes. This is called an examen or examination of conscience. Ask yourself: Did I lie today? Was I honest in my dealings? Did I treat people with respect or did I use anyone? Did I compromise my values to fit in? This daily check-in, done in God's presence, keeps your conscience sharp. When you identify a lapse, resolve to make it right (if you lied, correct it; if you mistreated someone, apologize) and bring it to confession if serious. This way, you don't drift far off course; you correct your moral direction daily, much like a pilot making frequent minor adjustments to stay on course to his destination. Also, seek out good formation. Read Catholic literature on moral issues, especially areas you find confusing. The Church has rich teachings on bioethics, social justice, sexual ethics, etc. that can guide you. Don't rely solely on secular media or internet chatter to form your views, go to the sources: Scripture, Catechism, encyclicals, and trusted Catholic authors. When a tough moral question arises (say, something like, "Is it ever okay to withhold medical treatments?" or "How do I balance charity with not enabling someone?"), you can research what wise Christian minds have said. This not only gives you answers, but also trains you in the art of moral reasoning. Over time, you'll gain confidence that your conscience is reliable because it's well-founded on truth. And that confidence enables you to act decisively and peacefully when confronted with ethical dilemmas. Reflection: Think of a time you felt torn between doing what was right and taking an easier or more popular path. How did you respond, and what does that reveal about the formation of your conscience? Are there areas in your life now where you feel a nagging unease, suspecting you might not be aligning with God's moral law (perhaps in business, in what you watch, or how you treat someone)? Reflect on what influences have shaped your sense of right and wrong the most—was it your family, peers, media, or the Church's teaching? Where might you need to "re-calibrate" your conscience to point more truly to God's truth? Action Steps:

Conscience Examination: This week, perform a nightly examination of conscience. It can be brief (5-10 minutes). Use the Ten Commandments or the Beatitudes as a framework, or even the simple questions: Did I love God today? Did I love my neighbour as myself today? Note any moments of failure or discomfort. At the end of the week, observe any patterns (e.g., frequent small lies, impatience, etc.) that need addressing.

Clarify a Value: Identify one moral principle you hold (for example, "honesty in all dealings" or "chastity until marriage" or "fairness in business"). Write a short paragraph on why you believe it's the right thing, backing it up with a Scripture or Church teaching reference. This exercise strengthens your understanding and resolve. If someone were to challenge you on this point, you'll be more prepared to articulate and stand by it.

Truth in Speech: Practice eliminating "little lies" and exaggerations in your daily speech. Challenge yourself to a week of complete honesty (with charity). If you usually say "I'll be there in 5" but know it's 15, speak the truth. If you catch yourself lying, immediately correct it ("Actually, let me rephrase, the truth is…"). This will make you more aware of how easy it is to slip, and how living truthfully requires vigilance.

Learn the Church's Teaching: Pick a topic you're unsure or curious about morally (such as contraception, just war, social justice, etc.). This week, find a reliable Catholic resource (the Catechism or a Catholic Answers article, for instance) and read what the Church teaches and the reasoning behind it. Share what you learn with a friend or your spouse. Teaching someone else is a great way to solidify your own understanding and commitment.

Chapter 5: Sacred Sexuality – Living Pure in a Pornified Culture

The Fortress Within

The Fortress Within

Narrative: Tom's story could be the story of countless men. He was 13 when he first stumbled upon internet pornography on a home computer. What began as curiosity turned into a secret habit through high school and college. By the time Tom was a young adult, he found he couldn't go more than a few days without seeking out explicit images or videos. On one hand, he knew it was wrong and felt ashamed; on the other hand, he rationalized, "I'm not hurting anyone. It's just pixels on a screen." When Tom started dating a wonderful woman, he assumed marriage would automatically cure the problem. But it didn't. The habit followed him into married life, undermining his intimacy with his wife. He found himself less attracted to real intimacy and more drawn to fantasy. Eventually, his wife discovered his secret. It was a painful wake-up call. Tom had to face the fact that pornography had become an addiction and was indeed hurting both him and the person he loved most. With humility, he sought help: confession with a wise priest, accountability software on his devices, and a Christian support group for men. It wasn't an overnight fix, but over time, through prayer, penance, and openness, Tom broke free from the chains of porn. His marriage began to heal as he relearned how to truly love and respect. Tom's journey shows both the depth of the struggle and the hope of redemption. We live in a culture soaked in lust, but with God's grace, we can live in purity. God's Design for Sexuality: Let's start with the positive vision. Why does purity matter so much? Because human sexuality is sacred. God designed it to be an expression of love so profound that it creates life and bonds spouses into one flesh (cf. Genesis 2:24). In Catholic teaching, the sexual act is a holy gift reserved for the covenant of marriage between one man and one woman, open to the possibility of life and sealed by the mutual self-gift of the spouses. In that context, sex is not only physically pleasurable but spiritually meaningful, a participation in God's creative love. The pleasure is meant to be the icing on the cake of a much deeper union that involves the whole person: body, mind, and soul. When sex is removed from this sacred context, its power, instead of bonding in love, can become destructive. The world around us has largely severed sex from marriage, love from responsibility, pleasure from purpose. The results are everywhere: broken hearts, broken families, objectification of persons (especially women), and an epidemic of addiction to lust in various forms. The pornography industry, now readily accessible on every smartphone, is one of the greatest distorters of God's plan. It takes what is beautiful, the human body and marital intimacy, and perverts it into a consumable product. People (often those trapped in the industry by coercion or desperation) become objects to be used rather than persons to be loved. As Pope John Paul II emphasized in his Theology of the Body, the opposite of love is not hate, but use, treating a person as an object for gratification rather than as someone with infinite dignity. The Battle for Purity: Given this cultural onslaught, living chastely is a real battle. Chastity means the successful integration of sexuality within the person; in other words, it's a virtue that enables us to express our sexual desires in healthy, holy ways according to our state in life (married or single). For a single man, chastity means refraining from sexual acts and guarding one's mind and heart from lust. For a married man, chastity means faithfulness to your wife, both physically and mentally, and treating her with respect and love, never as a mere outlet for lust. In both cases, it involves discipline of eyes and thoughts, not just actions. Let's be frank: temptations against purity are everywhere, provocative images in ads, suggestive content in movies and music, social media feeds algorithmically feeding lustful content, and the normalization of premarital sex and pornography. It can feel like trying to stay dry in a rainstorm. But consider this: if something is valuable, it's worth protecting. You would guard a precious jewel carefully; how much more should we guard the purity of our hearts and the sanctity of our relationships? Jesus gave strong warnings about lust. He said, "Everyone who looks at a woman with lust has already committed adultery with her in his heart" (Matthew 5:28). And, "If your right hand causes you to sin, cut it off... it is better for you to lose one of your members than for your whole body to go into hell" (Matt 5:30). He wasn't advocating literal self-mutilation; He was using shocking imagery to tell us to take radical measures to avoid sin. In practice, that might mean "cutting off" access to temptation: installing blockers on devices, avoiding certain websites or media, even ending a toxic relationship that's leading to sin.

Healing the Eyes and Heart: Purity isn't just about repressing urges; it's about re-training our eyes and heart to see rightly. We must learn to see others not as objects, but as persons, brothers and sisters, fellow children of God. This requires prayer and grace. A beautiful practice is to pray for the people who tempt you, literally, if an immodestly dressed person or a seductive image crosses your path, instead of indulging or cursing the temptation, say a quick prayer: "Lord, bless that person" or "Lord, help me see Your child, not an object." This transforms the moment into one of love rather than lust. It's also crucial to fill your mind with what is good and true. Philippians 4:8 says, "Whatever is true, honourable, just, pure, lovely... think about these things." You might need to detox from the constant flow of sexualized entertainment. Take breaks from social media or shows that trigger lust. Replace them with wholesome content or hobbies that uplift you. Many men find that when they immerse themselves in prayer, meaningful work, exercise, and real-life connections, the power of pornography and fantasy weakens. Idle time and boredom can be dangerous; staying constructively engaged leaves less room for temptation to fester. Specific Strategies for Sexual Integrity: We have already talked about frequent Confession and the Eucharist, these are essential. In Confession, not only are your sins forgiven, but you receive grace to resist in the future. Don't be ashamed to bring impurity to Confession; priests have helped many through this battle and will not be shocked. Develop an accountability system: maybe an accountability partner or a support group. Knowing that someone else will ask you, "How are you doing with purity?" can fortify your resolve in weak moments. Use technology wisely: there are software programs that can filter content and send a report of your online activity to an accountability partner. These are tools that humble us but also protect us, especially in the critical period of breaking free from addiction. Prayer is your strongest weapon. In particular, many men struggling with impurity have found tremendous help in devotion to the Blessed Virgin Mary. Why Mary? Because she is the model of pure humanity, a loving mother who wants to keep her sons safe from sin. Praying the Rosary regularly is like taking a shower for the mind, it washes away a lot of the dirty images and strengthens you internally. It's been famously said that a man who prays the Rosary either will give up sin or give up the Rosary, because the two can't coexist for long. Also consider prayers like the St. Michael Prayer when feeling attacked, and simply calling on the name of Jesus (which carries power against evil). Some find it helpful to place sacred art or crucifix in their workspace or bedroom as a visual reminder of the holy. If you're married, invest in genuine intimacy with your wife. That includes emotional connection: listening, spending quality time, praying together. Often, problems like pornography arise or persist in marriage when spouses drift apart emotionally or are under stress. By proactively nurturing your marriage, through date nights, honest conversation, affection, you strengthen the bond that satisfies the heart, leaving less room for temptations. Also practice custody of the eyes out of respect for your wife; make that covenant with your eyes (Job 31:1) to not gaze lustfully at others. It honours her and keeps your heart undivided. For those not yet married, know that chastity now is possible and incredibly beneficial. It trains you to love authentically. You're proving by self-control that you can sacrifice for the good of another, which is the essence of love. Many happily married couples will attest that the effort to remain chaste before marriage built trust and respect that paid dividends later. If you've fallen in this area, don't despair, seek forgiveness and start anew. God can restore purity of heart. Remember Jesus' encounter with the woman caught in adultery (John 8): He did not condemn her, but told her, "Go and sin no more." The Lord always offers a fresh start and the grace to live differently. The Rewards of Purity: Living purely isn't just about avoiding negative consequences; it brings great blessings. Jesus promised, "Blessed are the pure of heart, for they shall see God" (Matthew 5:8). Purity of heart enables us to perceive God's presence more clearly and to experience deeper peace. Men who break free from lust report a new clarity of mind, better relationships, and a sense of self-mastery that boosts confidence. Your capacity to truly love increases, whether it's love for your spouse, your kids, or friends, in purity you can will the good of the other without selfish taint. You become, as the title of this book suggests, a fortress, strong and secure, rather than a city with broken walls that any passion can overrun (cf. Proverbs 25:28).

The Fortress Within

And should God call you to marriage, the virtue of chastity will make you a far better husband and father. If He calls you to remain single or to religious life, chastity will enable you to channel your energies into fruitful service and relationships. In all cases, purity is tied to freedom: freedom to love without chains of addiction or guilt, freedom to look anyone in the eye without shame, freedom to worship God with an undivided heart. Reflection: Examine your life in terms of purity. Are there habits, media, or relationships that consistently pull you toward lust or sexual sin? How do you respond to those temptations currently, with resistance, indifference, or surrender? Consider how you view members of the opposite sex: do you see them as persons or sometimes catch yourself reducing them to objects? Be honest about the impact lust may be having on your spiritual life, your self-respect, or your relationships. How might your life be different if you were free from any impure habits or guilt? Allow yourself to imagine the peace and strength that would bring, and let that motivate you to pursue it. Action Steps:

Clean House (Digital Purity): Do an audit of your digital life. Remove or block sources of temptation: uninstall apps that lead you to stumble, set up a content filter on your phone and computer (many are free or low-cost), and unfollow social media accounts that regularly post impure content. This is like removing the "near occasion of sin" in modern form.

Accountability: Choose a trustworthy friend (or a support group, or a counsellor if needed) and have a frank conversation about your commitment to purity. Ask them to check in on you, or consider pairing up with another man who is actively trying to grow in purity, agreeing to encourage and pray for each other. Sometimes just knowing someone will ask, "How are you doing with this?" can help you in moments of temptation.

Daily Devotion for Purity: For the next month, incorporate a daily spiritual practice specifically for purity. For example: pray three Hail Marys every morning for purity (a traditional practice recommended by many saints) or pray a decade of the Rosary specifically for those ensnared in pornography (this intention also humbles you to remember you rely on grace). You could also read a few pages of a book on Theology of the Body or a saint's writings on chastity each day to inspire you. Consistency here is key.

Date with God or Spouse: If single, dedicate one night a week as "date night with God" go to Adoration or find a quiet place to read Scripture, treating that time as sacred. If married, plan a special date night with your wife within the next two weeks, focused on reconnection (no phones, perhaps a heartfelt conversation where you also apologize for any ways lust or distractions have hurt your unity). Strengthening your primary relationship (with God or your wife) is one of the best guards against illicit desires.

Chapter 6: Courage and Conviction – Standing for What's Right

[59]

The Fortress Within

Narrative: A colleague once shared a story with me from early in their career that really stuck. In their own words: I recall a work trip early in my career when a few colleagues decided that after our conference sessions, the evening's entertainment would be a strip club. They cheerfully assumed everyone was on board. My heart sank, I knew this was against everything I believed about respecting women and staying pure, but I felt a knot of fear. What would they think of me if I said no? Would I seem uptight, lose their camaraderie, maybe even hurt my standing at the company? A silent prayer shot up: Lord, help me do the right thing. I mustered my courage and told them, as calmly as I could, "You guys go ahead, but I'm going to pass on this one." There was some awkward silence. One co-worker laughed like I must be joking. But when he saw I was serious, the teasing began: "Oh, come on, don't be such a saint! Live a little!" I simply repeated that I wasn't comfortable with it and headed back to the hotel. I'll be honest: walking away felt lonely. I spent that night alone, wondering if I'd just branded myself the office prude. But in my heart, amid the sting of their ridicule, I felt an unexpected peace. I knew I had chosen principle over popularity. Later, one colleague (who didn't join the others either for his own reasons) told me quietly that he respected my stance. That small affirmation felt like God's way of saying, "See, it was worth it." Standing up for what's right often does cost something, but it secures something far greater: a clear conscience and moral integrity. The Virtue of Fortitude: Courage, or fortitude, is one of the cardinal virtues and it's absolutely essential for living out our faith in the real world. Fortitude is the moral strength that enables us to endure difficulties and to remain steady in doing the good, even when it's unpopular or dangerous. We tend to think of courage as not having fear, but in truth, courage is feeling the fear and doing the right thing anyway. In a "compromised world" where many people prefer to go with the flow, a man of conviction will often stand out, sometimes uncomfortably so. Consider the example of Saint Thomas More, a 16th-century English statesman. When King Henry VIII demanded that everyone acknowledge him (and not the Pope) as head of the Church so he could divorce and remarry, Thomas More, a close advisor to the King, refused. He knew it would cost him dearly, indeed, it cost him his life. Before his execution, Thomas declared, "I die the King's good servant, but God's first." His courage to stand for truth over royal pressure made him a martyr and a saint. Now, most of us won't face execution for our faith (thank God), but we each have our moments where we must choose: serve God first, or bend to the pressures of the crowd or authority. It could be as small as laughing along at a bigoted or lewd joke to fit in, or as significant as risking your job by refusing to commit fraud or to participate in something against your beliefs. These moments test our resolve: will we be men of integrity or men of expedience? Integrity in Action: Courage is closely tied to integrity, being consistent in our moral principles no matter the setting. A man of integrity doesn't leave his faith or values at the church door on Sunday; he carries them into his workplace, his social life, everywhere. This doesn't mean he's preachy or self-righteous; it means he's authentic and principled. If you value honesty, you won't lie on a report even if your boss suggests it. If you value chastity, you won't cheat on your wife even if an opportunity presents itself. If you value kindness, you'll speak up when someone is being bullied or maligned, rather than silently allowing it. Integrity often requires speaking up or acting when it would be easier to stay silent or do nothing. It might mean being the one to say, "This isn't right" when everyone else is going along with wrongdoing. One challenge we face is the fear of human respect—essentially, caring too much about what others think. It's natural to want to be liked and to get along with peers, neighbours, and colleagues. But sometimes this desire becomes a trap. We might compromise on our values to avoid conflict or to gain approval. Jesus anticipated this when He said, "Woe to you when all men speak well of you" (Luke 6:26), indicating that if we never face opposition, we might not be truly living the radical call of the Gospel. He also comforted us with, "Blessed are those who are persecuted for righteousness' sake, for theirs is the kingdom of heaven" (Matthew 5:10). While we may not want to think of ourselves as facing "persecution", even mild social backlash for doing right is a share in that beatitude. And God sees and rewards the sacrifices we make for the sake of goodness. Picking Your Battles and Fighting the Right Way: Standing for what's right doesn't mean being combative about everything. Prudence (wise judgment) helps us know when and how to take a stand. Not every disagreement at work or home needs to turn into a moral showdown. Some hills are not worth dying on; others absolutely are. A prudent man discerns which issues are core principles that can't be compromised (like honesty, protecting the innocent, fidelity to faith) and which issues might allow some flexibility or patient dialogue. When you do take a stand, how you do it matters. Screaming or insulting others, or acting with arrogance, can undermine your witness. Instead, speak the truth with love and respect. For example, if you need to voice opposition to an unethical policy at work, you might calmly explain your ethical concern and propose an alternative if possible, rather than just saying "You're all wrong!" and storming out. Sometimes your courage will win others over; other times it won't, but at least you won't give unnecessary offense that obscures the issue. Relying on Faith: Where do we find courage when our knees are knocking? Ultimately, from our faith in God. David facing Goliath declared, "The battle is the Lord's" (1 Samuel 17:47). If you know you are doing what's right in God's eyes, you can trust that He will back you up, maybe not by stopping all consequences, but by working all things for good in the end (Romans 8:28). There's a tremendous freedom in leaving the results to God. You can say, "Lord, I will stand for the truth; I trust You with what comes next." This trust enables martyrs to sing in prison cells and everyday heroes to endure being the odd one out without bitterness. Also, remember the support of fellow believers. When Elijah thought he was the only faithful one left in Israel, God revealed there were 7,000 others who hadn't bowed to idols (1 Kings 19:14-18). You are not alone. There are other men and women of faith in your community, parish, and indeed in your workplace or extended family who share your values. Finding allies can bolster your courage. Even one friend who supports you can make a difference (as my colleague experienced with his colleague who later respected his stance). And even if you truly stand alone among humans, you stand with Christ, who Himself stood alone before Pilate and the jeering crowds, witnessing to the truth. He is with you in those moments in a profound way, saying, "Take courage, it is I; do not be afraid" (Matthew 14:27). Everyday Acts of Courage: While some acts of courage are big and dramatic, most are smaller and quieter but no less important to God. It might be the courage to admit you made a mistake at work rather than covering it up. Or the courage to lovingly correct a friend who is engaging in self-destructive behaviour. Or the courage to refuse to watch a popular show that everyone is raving about because you know it's morally offensive. Or the courage as a father to say "no" to your kids about something all their friends are doing, and then patiently explaining why. These daily decisions to live with integrity form a habit of courage. And like a muscle, your courage grows each time you use it. Over time, people will come to know that you are a man who means what he says and stands by what he believes.

[64]

Interestingly, while some may mock that, many others will quietly admire and even rely on it. You might become the person they turn to when they need honest advice or someone they can trust precisely because you've shown you won't bend with the wind. Reflection: When was the last time you stood up for a principle despite risk? Is there some situation now calling you to show moral courage? If so, what's the worst that could happen if you do the right thing, and what's the worst that could happen if you don't? Which can you live with? Reflect on the value of a clear conscience compared to the discomfort of others' disapproval. Ask God to reveal any area where fear is keeping you from doing what you know is right. Action Steps:

Micro-Courage Practice: This week, do something small that requires moral courage. It could be as simple as expressing a contrary (but truthful) opinion in a conversation where you'd normally just nod along. Or gently calling out a friend who tells an inappropriate joke: "Hey, that joke's a bit over the line." These low-stakes exercises build your courage muscles for bigger tests. Reflect on the outcome; you may find people respect you more, not less.

Set Your Boundaries in Advance: Identify a few moral lines you will not cross (e.g., "I will not lie on official documents," "I will not betray my marriage vows," "I will not assist in something gravely unethical at work," etc.). Write them down. By deciding in advance, you're more prepared when a situation arises. It's easier to be brave when you're not caught off-guard. Pray over these commitments and ask God to fortify you for each scenario.

Find a Role Model: Learn about a saint or modern figure known for moral courage. For example, read about St. Thomas More, St. Joan of Arc, or modern martyrs like St. Oscar Romero. Or even a contemporary like a whistleblower who stood up for what was right. Draw inspiration from their stories and identify what enabled them to be brave (faith, prayer, conviction). Ask for that saint's intercession when you need courage.

Support Someone Else: If you know someone who is taking a principled stand (maybe a friend refusing to compromise at work, or a family member making a tough moral choice), reach out with encouragement. Being a source of support for another not only helps them; it reinforces in you the value of courageous integrity. It's easier to be brave when we bolster each other. Plus, you create a culture of courage around you, which can make doing the right thing feel less like lone combat and more like a shared endeavour.

Part III: Financial Discipline – Building a Legacy, Not Just Wealth

"For what does it profit a man to gain the whole world and forfeit his soul?" (Mark 8:36)

Chapter 7: God's Money, God's Mission – Embracing Stewardship

[69]

The Fortress Within

Narrative: John had always equated success with the size of his bank account. He worked relentless 60-hour weeks, climbing the corporate ladder and investing shrewdly. By age 45, he had a luxury car, a big house, and a sizable portfolio. But his relentless pursuit of wealth came at a cost, his marriage was strained, and he hardly knew his kids beyond quick greetings. Sundays were more for catching up on sleep or emails than for church or family time. John told himself it was all for them, to secure their future, but deep down he knew his identity was tied up in being "the provider" and having the best of everything. One day, John's father fell gravely ill. In his father's final days, he imparted some words that shook John: "Son, I regret spending so little time with you all while chasing my career. Don't make the same mistake with your kids. Money is useful, but it isn't everything." After his father passed, John reflected on those words. The man had left some money behind, but far more valuable were the love and life lessons he passed on. John realized he'd been chasing a hollow version of legacy. That week he dusted off the family Bible and stumbled on this verse: "The earth is the Lord's and everything in it" (Psalm 24:1). It dawned on him that all his wealth belonged to God; he was just a manager. In that moment, John's perspective on money transformed from ownership to stewardship. And with it, his approach to life and legacy began to change. Everything Belongs to God: The first principle of financial discipline for a Catholic man is recognizing that all we have is from God and ultimately belongs to God. We are stewards, not owner. This fundamental truth redefines prosperity: it's not about how much we accumulate, but how faithfully we use what God entrusts to us. King David prayed, "All things come from You, and of Your own have we given You" (1 Chronicles 29:14). In other words, whenever we give or do good with our resources, we're just returning a portion of what was God's to begin with. Such a perspective is radically different from the secular view. Secular society often says, "You earned it, it's yours to do whatever you please." But the Catholic perspective frames wealth as a tool for a higher purpose. It doesn't mean you can't enjoy any fruits of your labour or provide comfort for your family, of course you should provide and it's okay to enjoy legitimate blessings. However, we hold our material possessions loosely, ready to use them for God's mission and the good of others, not just our own pleasure. This attitude guards us against the idol of greed. Jesus warned, "Take care! Be on your guard against all kinds of greed; for one's life does not consist in the abundance of possessions" (Luke 12:15). He then told a parable of a rich fool who stored up grain but died before he could enjoy it, concluding, "So it is with those who store up treasures for themselves but are not rich toward God" (Luke 12:21). To be "rich toward God" means investing in (Continued) To be "rich toward God" means investing in things of eternal value, not just padding our net worth. Called to Stewardship: Stewardship means we manage God's gifts responsibly. This includes money, but also time, talents, and the created world. Focusing on money: being a steward has several implications:

We provide for our family's needs (this is a moral duty – "If anyone does not provide for his relatives... he has denied the faith", 1 Timothy 5:8).

We use our resources to help those in need and support the Church's mission (generosity).

We avoid waste and undue extravagance, recognizing resources are precious.

We plan for the future prudently to ensure stability and care for loved ones (saving, investing ethically, etc.), but without anxiety, trusting ultimately in God's providence.

We make all financial decisions (big and small) in light of our values, not in isolation from them (e.g., refusing to earn money in unethical ways, or avoiding investments that fund immoral industry). In practice, this could mean setting a family budget that reflects your priorities. For example, maybe you choose a modest vacation so that you can also afford to donate to a charity or pay Catholic school tuition. It might mean career choices, perhaps turning down a higher-paying job that would demand you compromise family time or ethics. These choices can be tough, but remember Jesus' promise: "Seek first the kingdom of God and His righteousness, and all these things will be given you as well" (Matthew 6:33). If you put God's priorities first, He will ensure your needs (not necessarily every want) are met. Wealth as a Tool for Good: Money in itself is neither evil nor good; it's a tool. The love of money is the root of evil (1 Timothy 6:10), not money per se. When we see money as a means to fulfil God's purposes, providing for family, helping others, building up society, we approach it virtuously. Catholic social teaching emphasizes the universal destination of goods, meaning God intended the goods of creation for every person's benefit. This challenges us to use our excess to aid those who lack basics. If God has blessed you with steady income or wealth, it's not just for your own comfort. He's entrusting you with the opportunity to bless others. One concrete way to live this is through tithing and charitable giving. The ancient biblical concept of tithing (giving 10% of one's income) is a benchmark many Christians strive for. The Catholic Church doesn't mandate a strict percentage, but we are called to support the Church and the poor according to our ability. Giving a planned portion of our income (whether 5%, 10%, or more) back to God, through the Church and charities, is a powerful spiritual practice. It reminds us that our money is ultimately not ours. It trains us in trust, that God can do more with the 90% we keep than we could do with 100% without His blessing. As one Catholic businessman put it, "When I made God my partner through tithing, I found my business actually thrived more." While not a get-rich scheme, it does align with God's promise that "Whoever sows generously will also reap generously" (2 Corinthians 9:6). The blessings might be material or they might be spiritual, like greater contentment and less attachment to material things. If a full tithe is hard for you right now, start smaller but make it regular, and then challenge yourself to increase as you're able. Make a budget that includes giving, not as the last category (what's left over), but as a priority (first fruits). And giving isn't only writing checks, also consider your time and skills as currencies for God's work (volunteering at church, helping a neighbour with repairs, etc.). Providing Versus Hoarding: Being a good steward also means prudent saving and planning. Yes, be generous, but also ensure you're fulfilling responsibilities like having an emergency fund, saving for children's education if applicable, and preparing for retirement. The key difference between prudent saving and hoarding is your attitude and purpose. Are you saving out of wisdom or out of fear/greed? Do you have a reasonable goal, or is it never enough? Jesus advises planning (Luke 14:28-30), but He also warned against the rich fool who hoarded and found it was all for naught. Strike a balance: set savings goals that make sense, but once met, consider if further accumulation is necessary or if it can be directed to other needs. Another aspect of stewardship is ethical earning. Ask yourself: is my way of making money in line with my faith? A classic example: a man might refuse a lucrative job that requires dishonesty or exploitation. Or an investor might choose funds that avoid profiting from, say, pornography, abortion or other immoral industry. These choices can be countercultural (because it might mean less profit), but they witness that we put conscience above cash. God can honour such sacrifices in surprising ways. Remember, "Better is a little with righteousness than great revenues with injustice" (Proverbs 16:8). Family and Finances: As a Catholic man, especially if you're a husband/father, your stewardship extends to how you lead your family in financial matters. Money is a common source of stress in households; part of building a legacy is creating a healthy financial culture at home. This means communicating openly with your spouse about budget and goals, teaching your children about money (like the value of work, saving, and charity, and making family decisions that prioritize faith and virtue over keeping up with the Joneses. For example, choosing to live in a slightly smaller house so that mom or dad can have more time with the kids (rather than working overtime for a bigger mortgage) is a value-based decision. Or turning down certain social events that revolve around material showiness. These send a message to your family: We use money, but we don't serve money. Involving kids in charitable giving can be a powerful lesson. Perhaps have a family charity jar where you all contribute spare change and decide together where to donate it. Or involve them when you deliver food to a food pantry. This shows them from early on that part of handling money is to bless others. Also, let them see you writing the check or hitting "send" on the donation to your parish or charity; these small observations stick with children and normalize generosity. Contentment and Trust: A huge part of financial discipline is learning contentment. Our consumer culture thrives on stoking dissatisfaction, convincing us we need the latest gadget, car, or fashion to be happy. But if we constantly chase more, we'll never rest and always risk financial trouble. St. Paul said, "I have learned in whatever state I am, to be content" (Philippians 4:11). That is a goal to aspire to. Contentment doesn't mean lack of ambition; it means gratitude for what you have and a sense of sufficiency. When we practice contentment, it's easier to live within our means, avoid excessive debt, and say no to purchases that aren't necessary. It frees us from the comparison game that often drives people into unsustainable spending. Underlying all this is trust in God's providence. If you are doing your part, working diligently, living within your means, being generous, trust that God will provide for you. This trust can liberate you from excessive worry about money. So many men carry the quiet anxiety of "Will I have enough? Will my family be okay?" Planning and insurance can mitigate some risks, but ultimately our security comes from God. Jesus invites us to look at the birds and the flowers that God feeds and clothes, and not to be anxious (Matthew 6:25-30). By all means, have a financial plan, but submit it to God and acknowledge Him as your true source. This humility and trust keep wealth in its proper place, as a means, not an end. Reflection: How do you view money and success? Do you find security in your bank balance or in God's presence? Reflect on your spending patterns: do they align with what you say your priorities are (faith, family, service)? Are there ways in which money has too strong a grip on your heart, perhaps an attachment to luxury, or constant worry about finances, or reluctance to be generous? Conversely, consider the blessings you have received: how have you seen God provide for you at different points in life? In what ways could you be a more faithful steward of the gifts (money, possessions, talents) entrusted to you? Action Steps:

Gratitude Inventory: Make a list of all the material and financial blessings in your life (income, house, food, etc.). Then say a prayer of thanksgiving, explicitly acknowledging each as a gift from God. Do this whenever you feel discontentment creeping in, it will shift your mindset from entitlement to gratitude.

Review Your Budget/Spending: If you don't have a budget, create a simple one; if you do, review it. Identify categories: giving, savings, essentials, discretionary. Aim to allocate a percentage to giving (even if small to start) and treat it like a bill you owe God (in gratitude). Look at discretionary spending (e.g., eating out, entertainment) and see if it reflects your values or if adjustments are needed. Discuss these with your spouse if applicable.

Set a Family Financial Value: For instance, "Our family values generosity over luxury" or "We live simply so others can simply live." Write it down and perhaps put it on the fridge or family bulletin board. Make a concrete goal tied to it, like reducing a certain expense to increase charitable giving or family time. Having a motto helps align everyone to the mission.

Act of Generosity: Do one concrete generous act that stretches you a bit. It could be donating to a charity an amount that makes you slightly uncomfortable (in the sense that you notice the sacrifice), or buying a meal for someone in need, or giving away possessions you don't truly need. Do it privately, as an offering to God. Notice the joy or freedom that can come from letting go. As Jesus said, "It is more blessed to give than to receive" (Acts 20:35). Experiencing that blessedness will encourage more of it and slowly loosen any hold greed may have on you.

Chapter 8: Discipline and Diligence – Mastering Your Finances

The Fortress Within

The Fortress Within

Narrative: Carlos never considered himself bad with money, but he also never really tracked it. He worked hard and earned decently, so he figured things would take care of themselves. That illusion shattered one embarrassing day at the grocery store. His card was declined. Assuming a mistake, he tried another card, declined. With people in line behind him, he shuffled out of the store, groceries left behind. At home, Carlos and his wife opened their bills and faced the truth: they were in deep credit card debt and living pay check to pay check. How did this happen? Little by little: the new furniture on an instalment plan, dining out several times a week, the spontaneous weekend getaway they "deserved" after a tough month, all on plastic. They realized they had to change, fast. That night, they started learning about budgeting. It was humbling, like putting their entire financial life under a microscope. But it was also empowering. They set a goal to be debt-free in two years and laid out a plan: cutting cable, cancelling unnecessary subscriptions, cooking at home, selling the second car. The first month was hard as they adjusted to simpler living, but when they paid off the first credit card entirely, they felt a surge of accomplishment. Carlos said it felt like they got a raise just by managing money better. Over time, budgeting became second nature. They told their money where to go instead of wondering where it went. The discipline that seemed painful at first turned into a source of peace and even unity in their marriage as they worked together toward their goals. Living Within Your Means: Financial discipline starts with the basic principle:

spend less than you earn. It sounds obvious, yet so many of us struggle because credit makes it easy to spend more than we have. To live within your means, you must know what your means are, this is where budgeting comes in. A budget is simply a plan for your money. It's not about depriving yourself; it's about being intentional. Think of a budget as a tool to help you exercise the virtues of prudence and temperance with finances. Instead of money leaking out here and there, you capture it on paper (or a spreadsheet) and assign it purposefully. If you've never budgeted, start by tracking every expense for a month. It can be eye-opening. You might discover, for instance, that those small daily coffee purchases add up to £100 a month, or that streaming subscriptions you rarely use are bleeding funds. Once you see where money is going, you can categorize needs vs wants. Ensure essentials are covered: housing, food, utilities, transportation, insurance, these come first. Then allocate for debts, savings, and giving. Finally, see what's left for discretionary "fun" spending. Often, the exercise reveals that a bit of cutting back in non-essentials can free up money to meet goals that truly matter (like getting out of debt or investing in the kids' education). Avoiding the Debt Trap: Not all debt is equal. A reasonable mortgage on a modest home or a student loan for a useful degree can be investments in your future. But high-interest consumer debt (credit cards, personal loans for lifestyle upgrades) can enslave us. The Bible says, "The borrower is slave to the lender" (Proverbs 22:7). Many men lose sleep under the weight of debt. If you are in that situation, make it a priority to break free. It may require radical changes for a season, but it is immensely freeing. List your debts (type, amount, interest rate). Form a strategy: some use the "debt snowball" (paying off smallest balances first for psychological wins), others the "debt avalanche" (tackling highest interest first for cost efficiency). Pick a method and stick to it. Celebrate each payoff milestone (in a budget-friendly way). Importantly, try not to take on new debt in the process, this might mean cutting up credit cards or leaving them at home to avoid impulse use. To avoid falling back into debt, cultivate patience and delayed gratification. The world markets everything as "buy now, pay later" or "you deserve it now." But often waiting and saving up changes your perspective, you may realize you don't need that item after all, or find a cheaper alternative. If you do use credit cards, treat them like cash: never charge more than you can pay off in full that month. If that's a temptation, stick to debit or cash until you build the habit. Smart Saving and Emergency Planning: Part of discipline is preparing for the unexpected. An emergency fund (even a starter goal of $1,000/£1,000, and then building to 3-6 months of expenses) is crucial. Without a cushion, any little car breakdown or medical bill goes straight onto a credit card, undoing progress. Make building an emergency fund one of your first savings goals. It provides peace of mind and prevents panic when life throws curveballs. After that, save for known future expenses (car replacement, home repairs) and long-term goals (retirement, kids' college). Automating savings can help you treat it like a non-negotiable "expense" that occurs every payday, moving money into savings/investments before you can spend it. Diligence at Work: Financial discipline isn't only about cutting spending; it's also about how we earn and increase our means through honest work. The Book of Proverbs is filled with praise for diligence and warnings against laziness: "The hand of the diligent will rule, while the slothful will be put to forced labour" (Prove 12:24). As a Catholic man, carrying out your work with integrity and excellence is part of your stewardship. Not only does it likely lead to better financial stability (promotions, opportunities, etc.), but it's also a witness. Being known as reliable, hardworking, and ethical at your job glorifies God. It doesn't mean becoming a workaholic (we must balance work with family and rest), but it means when you're on the job, you give it your best as if working for the Lord (Colossians 3:23). Sometimes improving your financial picture might involve getting additional training or education to qualify for better opportunities. That, too, can be part of stewardship, investing in your ability to provide. Just discern wisely and perhaps seek counsel: not every higher-paying path is worth taking if it contradicts your vocation or values (as we discussed earlier regarding integrity and family time). Battling Consumerism: We live in a consumer-driven society where advertisements constantly tempt us to buy more. One key to financial mastery is learning to say "enough." Our culture markets every new iteration of technology or fashion as a necessity, but we can practice "sober intoxication" of the Spirit by appreciating what we have. Embrace the idea of simple living. This doesn't mean living in poverty or never enjoying nice things; it means deliberately avoiding excess and unnecessary complication. For example, do you really need the latest phone upgrade every year? Do you need a brand new car, or will a reliable used one work? Can you vacation modestly instead of lavishly and still create great family memories? Choosing simpler options saves money that can go to debt repayment, savings, or charitable causes, and often, it reduces stress too. Many men find that decluttering their spending and possessions leads to a surprising sense of liberation. Communication and Teamwork: If you're married, financial discipline is a team sport. Both spouses should be on the same page about budget and goals; otherwise, it can breed resentment or sabotage. Have regular, calm discussions about money (some couples do a monthly budget night). Bring your shared values to the table: what kind of life do we want? What example do we set for our kids in how we use money? If you're single, you might find an accountability partner, a friend who also wants to be prudent financially; you can encourage each other to stick to budgets or savings plans. Balancing Work, Family, and Faith: Financial diligence includes balancing how we allocate our time, which is a non-renewable resource. It's possible to become so fixated on financial goals that we start to neglect family or faith, effectively making an idol of our financial plan. Watch out for that pitfall. If you find yourself constantly thinking about money, or regularly choosing extra work over essential family commitments for marginal financial gain, step back and re-evaluate. We practice discipline not for its own sake, but to enable a richer life in what matters most. Remember why you want financial stability in the first place, likely to reduce stress, to care for loved ones, to be free to serve God and others. Keep those reasons front and centre. We practice discipline not just to accumulate wealth, but to ensure our life, including our faith and relationships, flourishes. By mastering your finances, you're not just crunching numbers; you're exercising self-control, prudence, and responsibility. These virtues will spill over into other areas of your life too. You might find that as you become more organized with money, you become more organized with time management or more disciplined in personal habits like diet and exercise. Virtue tends to grow in clusters. Reflection: Consider your financial habits: are you generally disciplined or do you often feel money "disappears" without knowing where it went? How much stress does money (or lack thereof) cause in your life? If you carry debt, reflect on how it affects your freedom and peace of mind. Have you been procrastinating on addressing any financial issues (like a mounting debt or lack of savings)? Also, reflect on your work ethic: do you give your best at work and also know when to set boundaries for family and rest? Where do you see the virtue of temperance (self-control) at play in your financial life, and where could it be strengthened? Action Steps:

Start/Revise Your Budget: If you've never made a budget, create a simple one for the next month. List expected income and planned expenses (use past bank statements to estimate categories). (Conclusion)

If you end up with a negative balance, adjust by cutting some variable expenses. If you already budget, take an hour to refine it: does it realistically reflect current prices? Are you budgeting for irregular expenses (like car maintenance)? Update and adjust as needed, and commit to following it for the month.

Dealing with Debt: Write down your current debts (if any) with interest rates. Make a concrete plan to attack them: decide which debt to focus extra payments on first. Even if you can only add a small amount above minimums, start the process. Alternatively, if debt isn't an issue, consider if you're adequately saving; if not, redirect what would be a debt payment into a savings account monthly.

No-Spend Challenge: Challenge yourself (and your family, if applicable) to a "no-spend" period on non-essentials, maybe for one week or even a whole month. Buy only necessities (groceries, fuel, bills). Use the time to get creative: cook from your pantry, find free entertainment, etc. Track how much you save by the end. This exercise can reveal how much optional spending we do and help reset our habits.

The Fortress Within

Organize Important Documents: Part of financial discipline is managing what you have responsibly. Set aside time to organize your financial documents. Create or update a simple spreadsheet of accounts, bills, subscriptions, insurance policies, etc. Ensure you know interest rates, due dates, and have a plan for each. If you have a family, make sure your spouse knows where to find this information too. This step brings clarity and can highlight any "leaks" (like forgotten subscriptions or an insurance rate that could be lowered). Knowing exactly where you stand is half the battle in mastering your money.

Part IV: Integration – Living the Legacy Daily

"Be doers of the word, and not hearers only, deceiving yourselves." (James 1:22)

Chapter 10: Daily Disciplines – Crafting Your Rule of Life

The Fortress Within

Narrative: I'll admit it: for years, my daily life had no real plan or structure. I'd hit the snooze button multiple times, rush through the morning, and my prayers (if any) were squeezed in randomly. Evenings were often spent mindlessly scrolling on my phone or catching up on work I procrastinated on. I felt constantly "busy" yet also like I wasn't making progress on the things that mattered, especially spiritually. A friend suggested I try creating a "rule of life." The term made me think of monks in cloisters, so I was sceptical. But he explained that a rule of life is simply a schedule or set of habits that keep God at the centre and ensure you attend to your responsibilities in a balanced way. He challenged me: "Right now, you're living by default. What if you lived by design?" I took it to heart. Over the next few weeks, I prayerfully mapped out an ideal daily and weekly routine: set times for prayer, family, work, rest, exercise, etc. I posted this "rule" on my wall as a gentle guide. The change wasn't overnight or rigid, life still threw curveballs, but gradually I found a rhythm. I was actually praying consistently, getting enough sleep, and even had dedicated family time and personal study time. Far from feeling restrictive, the rule of life felt like a liberating structure that helped me become the man I wanted to be. He was right: instead of being tossed by the winds of each day's demands, I had an anchor and a sail. Why a Rule of Life? The term "rule" comes from the Latin regular, meaning a straight piece of wood, like a ruler that gives alignment. Monastic communities (like the Benedictines) have long used Rules to order their days toward prayer and work. But a rule of life isn't just for monks; it's for anyone who recognizes the need for structure to live out their values. Think of it as a personal covenant or blueprint that helps you allocate your time and energy in line with your priorities. Without intentional routines, good intentions often fall prey to the tyranny of the urgent or the lure of the easy. We've all experienced deciding to pray more or exercise more, but without a plan, those desires evaporate. A rule of life names the concrete practices you will live by. Paradoxically, following a rule can make you feel more free because you're not constantly reacting, you've proactively chosen how to spend your life. Elements of a Rule: Your rule of life will be unique to you (especially since each man's state in life and duties), but there are key elements every Catholic man should consider including:

Prayer: This is the cornerstone. Designate times for prayer. For example, commit to 15 minutes each morning for Scripture and prayer, maybe a decade of the Rosary on your commute, and a brief night prayer or examen. Schedule prayer like an important meeting with God, because it is. If you plan it, you're far more likely to do it.

Sacraments: Include Mass frequency (e.g., "Sunday Mass is absolute; try for one weekday Mass or Adoration weekly") and Confession (e.g., "Confession on first Saturday of the month") in your routine. Mark it on the calendar so it's anticipated, not a last-minute thought.

The Fortress Within

Work and Vocation: Block out your work hours, but also set boundaries around them so work doesn't spill over endlessly. If you're married, maybe you decide "no work emails after dinner." If single, perhaps dedicate certain evenings to ministry or family rather than extra office hours. Be intentional that your career serves your life mission, not vice versa.

Family & Relationships: Carve out time for those who matter most. It could be as simple as "family dinner at the table every night" or "Wednesday game night with the kids" or a weekly date night with your wife. If you're single, schedule regular visits or calls with parents/siblings, or time spent building wholesome friendships. These times should be protected from intrusion as much as possible.

Rest and Recreation: A rule isn't all "duties" it should also ensure you get proper rest and healthy recreation. Decide a consistent bedtime and wake-up that gives you enough sleep. Plan some leisure that recharges you (a hobby, reading, a sport) rather than mindless screen time. Even plan your weekly Sabbath (Sunday) with a mix of worship, family, and true rest, avoiding unnecessary work.

Health: Incorporate exercise and physical care into your routine. E.g., schedule a 30-minute walk or gym session thrice a week; plan meals to eat healthily; perhaps include fasting/abstinence on Fridays as a spiritual-health practice. A sound body supports a sound mind and soul.

Service/Charity: Include an element of serving others regularly. It might be volunteering monthly, or helping your parish weekly (like being an usher or catechist), or even simpler: checking on an elderly neighbour every Sunday. Building this in prevents your rule from becoming self-centred.

Personal Growth: Allocate time for learning (spiritual reading, listening to an inspiring podcast, studying something new related to your faith or profession). As men, we thrive when we're growing. Without planning, learning often gets sidelined. Maybe set 20 minutes before bed for reading, or a Saturday morning slot for an online course.

Digital Discipline: In our era, a rule of life should address technology. Set boundaries like "No phone during prayer and meals," or "Screen time off by 10 PM," or "One day a week unplugged from social media." This prevents tech from invading every moment and frees time for better things.

This may sound like a lot, but remember, your rule is a guide, not a rigid law. It exists to serve your ultimate goal (holiness and fulfilling your responsibilities), not to be an oppressive checklist. Also, implement changes gradually. If you currently have little structure, don't try to overhaul everything in one week. Introduce one or two elements, let them settle, then add more. Flexibility and Consistency: Life will throw curveballs—sickness, emergencies, special occasions. Your rule of life should have the flexibility to adapt without you feeling like a failure. Think of it like a trellis that guides a plant; if one branch grows differently, you gently train it back. If you miss your morning prayer because your child was sick overnight, find a moment later or start fresh tomorrow. Avoid the all-or-nothing mindset. Consistency is the aim, not perfection. Over time, you'll likely find that deviating from your rule (like oversleeping and skipping prayer) actually makes your day feel "off," which is a good sign that it's becoming a life-giving habit. And when everything is in chaos (vacation, holidays, upheavals), having an established rule even in minimal form (like still praying upon waking and before sleep) gives a sense of stability. One helpful practice is to periodically review your rule. Perhaps every few months, take an hour to assess: Is my rule helping me grow closer to God and love my family better? Where am I succeeding, and where am I consistently failing to live it? Maybe your schedule changed with a new job or a new baby, adjust the rule to fit the new reality. Remember, it's your servant, not your master. The goal is a balanced life where your priorities get the time they deserve. Living Intentionally: Integration is really about integrity, being whole and undivided. A well-crafted rule of life helps you integrate all the pieces of your identity: Catholic, husband, father, worker, friend, citizen. None of these gets neglected. It helps you avoid the common trap of compartmentalizing faith as just a Sunday thing; instead, it permeates your daily routine. You live the legacy daily by the small choices each day under a gentle discipline. As St. Francis de Sales advised, "Be regular and orderly in your life, so that you may be violent (i.e., passionate) in your love of God." The structure gives you the freedom to pour your energy into loving God and neighbour, rather than into scrambling to figure out your day. Reflection: Think about your typical day or week. Does it reflect your core priorities, or do urgent and trivial things often crowd out the important ones? Where do you waste the most time or feel most undisciplined? How might a more intentional routine help? Conversely, consider times when you had a good routine (maybe during Lent, or a period of training for an event) how did that affect your mood and growth? Are there elements like prayer or family time that you long to increase but "never find time" for? What would need to change to make room for them regularly? Action Steps:

Draft Your Rule: Set aside an evening or Sunday afternoon to write a first draft of your rule of life. Use the elements listed above as a checklist and fill in specific practices/times that work for you. It could be hourly ("6:30 AM rise and pray Morning Offering, 10 PM examine conscience...") or in blocks ("Morning routine: prayer, exercise; Work hours; Evening: family time, spiritual reading before bed" etc.). Don't worry about getting it perfect. Print or write it out and put it somewhere visible as a gentle reminder.

Start the Day Right: A great anchor for any rule is how you begin the day. Commit for the next two weeks to a fixed wake-up time (maybe even 15 minutes earlier than usual) and a simple morning routine that includes prayer first thing. This could be as simple as getting out of bed, kneeling and saying, "Good morning Lord, I offer You this day," then reading the Gospel of the day. Notice how this sets the tone for living deliberately rather than reactively.

One Change at a Time: Pick one area where lack of routine is hurting you and implement a change this week. For example: if you don't have a consistent meal with your family, designate at least two nights this week for a sit-down family dinner. Or if bedtime is chaotic and screens keep you up, set a "no screen after 10 PM" rule for yourself this week and use the time to wind down with prayer or reading. Focus on making that one change stick before adding another.

Accountability: Share your general plan or a specific part of your rule with someone you trust, a friend, your wife, or a men's group. For example, tell them, "I'm trying to pray the Rosary each day; can you check in with me next week on how it's going?" Knowing someone will ask helps motivate you to keep at it. Also, they might be inspired to join you in some aspects, and you can encourage each other. Living a rule of life is easier in community (even loosely) than completely alone.

Chapter 11: The Domestic Church – Leading Your Family by Example

[100]

The Fortress Within

Narrative: Michael had always assumed that as long as he took the family to Mass on Sunday, he was doing enough for his kids' faith. He left the teaching of religion to the parish school and the prayers to his devout wife. But when his older son, in his late teens, started drifting, skipping Mass, showing cynicism about the Church, Michael had a wake-up call. In a heart-to-heart, his son blurted out, "Why should I care about this stuff? It's not like we ever talk about God at home." The words stung because they were true. Faith was compartmentalized to Sunday mornings. Michael realized he'd been a passive bystander in the most important aspect of his family's life. He decided things needed to change: he would become the spiritual leader his family needed. It started small: he began saying grace more intentionally at dinner, then suggested a short night prayer with the family. He dusted off a family Bible and once a week after dinner, he read a passage and asked what the kids thought, sharing his own insights. He also began to gently share with his kids how God helped him in his daily struggles at work or with stress, something he'd never done before. Over months, the household atmosphere shifted. Discussions about faith became more natural. His teenager, seeing his dad's newfound sincerity, started engaging (even if with some eye-rolling at first). By the time his son went to college, he wasn't on fire with faith, but he was going to Mass of his own accord and even calling home to ask dad to pray for him during exams. Michael's decision to actively lead spiritually, rather than abdicate that role, had put his family on a firmer foundation. He learned that the domestic church thrives when the father steps into his role as its priestly leader. Your Home as a Church: The Second Vatican Council proclaimed, "The family is, so to speak, the domestic church. In it, parents should, by their word and example, be the first preachers of the faith to their children" (Lumen Gentium. This means your home is a microcosm of the universal Church, a place where God is worshiped, the faith is taught, and virtues are cultivated. As a Catholic man, and especially as a husband/father, you have a particular calling to shepherd this domestic church. Think of yourself (and your wife together) as the pastoral leaders of your little flock. This doesn't require theology degrees or saintly perfection. It requires love, intentionality, and leading by example. Priest, Prophet, King of the Home: Drawing from our baptismal identity and the example of Christ, a father is often analogized to being a priest, prophet, and king in his household. Not in a domineering sense, but in a service-oriented way:

Priest: A priest sanctifies and prays for his people. As the priest of your home, you are called to pray with and for your family. This might mean leading prayers at meals, initiating family rosaries or devotions, blessing your children (for instance, making the Sign of the Cross on their forehead at bedtime or before they head out for school), and ensuring the family receives the sacraments regularly. It also means offering sacrifices for them, perhaps fasting for a struggling child or bearing your own hardships with faith for their sake.

Prophet: A prophet teaches and bears witness to the truth. In the home, this means you actively share and teach the faith. It could be formally, like going over catechism lessons or discussing Sunday's Gospel, or informally, like bringing faith into everyday conversations ("Thank God for this good news" or "Let's trust the Lord with this problem"). It also means setting moral standards in the household, being clear about right and wrong and why (according to God's law). When kids have tough questions, the prophetic role means not shying away but engaging and guiding them to the truth, even if it's countercultural.

King: Christ the King leads by service and protects his people. In the family, the "kingly" role is about governance and protection. You set the spiritual tone and household policies that reflect your values (like establishing Sunday as a day for Mass and family, or deciding how to moderate TV/internet use to guard virtue). You protect your family from harmful influences, whether that's monitoring what media enters the home or intervening when a peer group is negatively impacting your child. As a servant-king, you also ensure the needs of the family are met: you work to provide, yes, but also ensure there is order, justice, and charity practiced at home.

It's powerful for children to see their father take faith seriously. It validates in their minds that "this is not just

[103]

something Mom cares about" or "just for women/kids." They see that being a man involves prayer, worship, and moral conviction. If you want your sons to be men of God and your daughters to seek men of God, show them what that looks like. Teamwork with Your Wife: If you're married, leading the domestic church is a joint effort with your wife. In many families, the mother has been the primary nurturer of faith, especially if she's more naturally inclined to prayer or spends more time with the kids. Your increased involvement isn't to overshadow her but to strengthen the overall spiritual support for the family. Talk with your wife about what faith practices she finds important and where she appreciates your leadership. Perhaps she's been hoping you'd take initiative in getting everyone to Mass or starting an Advent wreath tradition. Coordinate with her so you're on the same page. Presenting a united front reinforces to the children that faith is truly the centre of family life, not just one parent's interest. Family Practices: There are many ways to infuse faith into daily family life. Here are a few tried-and-true practices:

Daily Prayer Time: This could be morning or night prayers as a family. Some families do a brief Bible reading and decade of the Rosary in the evening. Others say an Our Father together before leaving for the day. Find a rhythm and keep it consistent.

Grace at Meals: Always pray before meals, even in public. It's a simple witness. Perhaps add a short thanksgiving after meals too (some families pray "We give Thee thanks..." in gratitude).

Blessings and Sacramentals: Utilize sacramentals. Have your home blessed by a priest. Use holy water, maybe have a little font by the door where family members can bless themselves each night. Enrol in the Brown Scapular or wear a blessed crucifix or medal and encourage your family to do likewise when ready, explaining their significance.

Liturgical Year at Home: Celebrate feasts and seasons. For example, light an Advent wreath and do a short prayer or hymn each week of Advent. Mark saints' feast days that are special to your family (patron saints of each member) with a special dessert or activity. This makes Catholicism joyful and woven into the fabric of life.

Service as a Family: Engage in charity together, as mentioned in earlier chapters. Perhaps make a tradition of volunteering occasionally or preparing a meal for a family in need. Let the kids participate. It teaches them that being Catholic is about love in action.

Open Conversations: Foster an environment where questions about faith are welcome. Perhaps during Sunday lunch you ask, "What did you get from the homily?" or "Any questions about the readings today?" Let them express doubts or curiosities without fear. If you don't know the answer, say, "Great question, let's find out together," and follow up. This shows humility and commitment to truth.

Extending Hospitality and Witness: Leading your family also has an outward dimension. Your home can be a place of hospitality and evangelization. Welcome other families or neighbours in, and let them see the warmth of your Christian family life. It doesn't mean being preachy to guests, but the way you say grace or have wholesome fun together can itself be a witness. Your children will also see that faith isn't something to hide, but to share naturally. Perhaps host a Bible study or a faith-sharing group at your home (if feasible) so your kids see spiritual conversation as a normal part of adult life. In doing so, you turn your domestic church into a small beacon in the community. When Family Members Aren't on Board: It's worth noting, you might face resistance. Perhaps your wife or teen isn't as enthusiastic. Lead gently. Don't start by mandating hour-long rosaries if that will cause rebellion. Begin with small, do-able practices and build. Let your genuine conviction and consistency do the talking. If you are a convert or recently reawakened Catholic and your family is used to the "old you" who wasn't devout, they might be sceptical. Show them through patience and love that this is a positive change, not a phase or fanaticism. Remember St. Peter's advice to wives about unbelieving husbands, that they may be won "without a word" by the conduct of their spouse (1 Peter 3:1-2). The principle applies generally: our lived example often speaks louder than lectures. So if family devotions are resisted, focus on personal example and one-on-one spiritual conversations first. And always pray for the Holy Spirit to move hearts (that's one area you lead invisibly as a priest of the home, constant intercession for your family). The Joyful Result: As you cultivate your domestic church, you'll likely notice a deeper unity in your family. Living faith together creates bonds that mere shared living under one roof doesn't. You'll also be giving your children the best chance to carry the faith forward. Even if some stray, the memory of a father who sincerely practiced what he preached will remain like a lighthouse beckoning them back. Leading your family spiritually is a sacred trust. God chose you specifically to father your children; He equips those He calls. Rely on that grace from the sacrament of marriage and the wisdom that comes from prayer. No family is perfect, but every family can strive to be a little church, a place where God is known and loved. By leading in this way, you truly "build the fortress" in the most important place, your home, brick by brick, day by day. Reflection: If you have a family, honestly assess: have you been actively leading them in faith, or more taking a back seat? How comfortable are you with praying aloud with your family or discussing faith? If it's uncomfortable, why, fear of awkwardness, feeling not knowledgeable enough? Consider what small step you could take to be a more present spiritual leader. Reflect on your family routines: what do they say about your family's priorities? Is God visibly a part of your home life or only implicitly? If you're single or without children, how can you contribute to the spiritual life of those around you (you might have siblings, nieces/nephews, or friends who look up to you)? We all have a sphere of influence, what example are you setting there? Action Steps:

Initiate Family Prayer: If you aren't doing this already, start with something simple like a nightly prayer together. For example, gather just before the kids' bedtime for a 5-minute prayer: an Our Father, each member can say one thing they're thankful for or need prayer for, then a Hail Mary. Keep it short, loving, and consistent. Over time, you can expand or add rosary decades or Scripture, but get the habit going first.

Faith on the Calendar: Plan at least one family faith activity in the next month. It could be attending a parish mission or retreat together, going on a pilgrimage to a nearby shrine for a day, or even having a movie night with a saint film and discussing it. Put it on the calendar as you would a sports game or school event. Show that faith events are a valued part of your family schedule.

Bless Your Children: Tonight, perhaps when they are going to bed, take a moment with each child, make a small Sign of the Cross on their forehead and say a short blessing (for example: "God bless you and keep you. May you sleep in His peace"). It might feel awkward if new, but most children (even teens, secretly) appreciate this gesture of love and spiritual care. Try doing this regularly (every night or at least before significant moments like exams, trips, etc.).

Family Meeting on Faith: If your kids are old enough, call a casual family meeting. Share with them that you've been thinking about how to grow as a family in faith. Solicit one idea from each person, make it a brainstorming game. You might hear suggestions like "let's pray a rosary when driving to Grandma's" or "what if we have donuts after Mass so we're excited to go" (they can be practical!). Implement at least one idea that surfaces. Involving them gives them ownership and shows that this is a family journey, not just dad imposing rules. Plus, you might be pleasantly surprised by their insights or enthusiasm.

Chapter 12: Never Fight Alone – Brotherhood and Ongoing Growth

[111]

The Fortress Within

Narrative: After a couple of years of striving to build his "fortress within," Alex felt both stronger and aware of his weaknesses more than ever. He had grown in prayer, cleaned up parts of his life, and was leading his family with new zeal. Yet, he occasionally hit walls of discouragement, old temptations flared up, or he'd slack off and feel guilty. He realized that while his personal commitment was solid, he was missing one element: brotherhood. He recalled how in college he had a tight-knit group of Catholic friends and how their camaraderie spurred him on. Now, as a busy 40-something, friendships had waned and most men he knew kept conversations at surface level. So, Alex took a bold step: he invited two guys from his parish, whom he admired, to start meeting once a week early in the morning for coffee and faith-sharing. They were surprisingly enthusiastic. What started as three men talking over the upcoming Sunday readings grew into a small band of brothers; in a few months, six or seven guys joined regularly. They prayed together, shared their struggles, and held each other accountable to the commitments they'd made (like sticking to prayer routines or overcoming bad habits). This fellowship became a lifeline for Alex. On days he felt weak or lazy, he'd remember his brothers and press on. When one of them overcame a hurdle, it inspired the rest. He came to understand deeply the proverb, *"As iron sharpens iron, so one man sharpens another. They were sharpening each other for the long journey of Christian manhood. The Long Haul: Building and living your legacy is not a one-time project; it's the work of a lifetime. There will be seasons of progress and seasons of setback. That's normal. What's important is persistence. St. Paul often used athletic metaphors: "Run with perseverance the race that is set before us" (Hebrews 12:1) and "I have fought the good fight, I have finished the race, I have kept the faith" (2 Timothy 4:7). God isn't interested in one-off spurts of zeal; He desires lifelong faithfulness. Perseverance is a virtue we need to intentionally cultivate. Part of that is learning to pick yourself up after failure (with God's grace in Confession) and not abandoning the quest because of discouragement or fatigue. Value of Brotherhood: We men often try to shoulder burdens alone, but Scripture and experience teach that we need brothers. Jesus sent out the apostles two by two; the early Christians formed tight communities. Having a band of faithful brothers can make the difference between flourishing and floundering. When you isolate yourself, you become more vulnerable to temptations and negative thoughts. But when you walk with others, you have additional eyes to see blind spots, additional hands to lift you when you fall, and companions to cheer you on. If you don't already have such fellowship, seek it out. Many parishes have men's groups, Bible studies, Knights of Columbus councils, or informal meet-ups. If not, maybe you are called to start one, even if it's just inviting a couple of friends as Alex did. Brotherhood provides accountability: For example, if you decide with a friend to both quit a bad habit (say, pornography or excessive drinking), you can check in and encourage each other. It also provides encouragement: your peers remind you that you're not crazy for striving to live virtuously in a world that often doesn't. And it provides camaraderie: it's just enjoyable and affirming to spend time with other men who share your faith and values, discussing everything from sports to the saints. Those bonds can sustain you in tough times. Consider joining or forming at least one circle of male fellowship as part of your rule of life. Even meeting once a month is a start. The key is to be known and to know others on the journey. Continuing Education: Another aspect of ongoing growth is to remain a learner. Never assume you've "arrived." There is always more to learn about God, about how to love your family, about virtues and even practical skills. Read good books (perhaps make it a point to read one solid Catholic or personal development book every few months). Attend retreats or conferences when you can; these can recharge your batteries and give fresh insight. Many men's retreats (like ACTS retreats, Cursillo, or parish missions geared to men) have sparked lasting change and networked men together. If you haven't been on one, consider making that a goal this year. Likewise, if your diocese or area has an annual Catholic men's conference, try to go; you'll experience the strength of hundreds or thousands of men worshiping together and hear inspiring talks. Mentorship is also a way to grow. Find a spiritual mentor or at least someone you look up to. It could be a priest, deacon, or just an older, wiser Catholic man. Meet with him periodically, ask questions, seek advice, and allow him to challenge you. And simultaneously, mentor those coming after you (as discussed in the legacy chapter). Teaching and guiding others has a way of solidifying our own commitments and knowledge. Navigating Setbacks: Perseverance doesn't mean never stumbling; it means when you stumble, you get back up. You may have seasons where prayer feels dry, or you slip into an old sin, or life circumstances (illness, job loss, etc.) upend your routines. In those moments, remember that the war is not won or lost in a day. Go back to basics: cling to the sacraments, even if you feel little consolation; lean on brothers to pray for you when you feel weak. If you fall into serious sin, do not stay down out of shame, go to Confession promptly, receive God's mercy, and start again. Our enemy wants to discourage us by making us think failures negate all progress. That is a lie. Often, progress is two steps forward, one step back. By God's grace, even those setbacks can teach humility and greater reliance on Him. Also, be patient with the growth of those around you. Perhaps you've made big changes in your life and you wish your brother or friend would "get with the program" too, but he's lagging. Pray for him and continue to be an example, but don't become judgmental or pushy to the point of straining relationships. Everyone's journey is unique. The best way to inspire others is by your joy and peace; show that this life of faith makes you a more alive, compassionate, and fulfilled man. That attracts others more than any lecture. Finishing Well: Keep your eyes on the finish line. One day, God-willing, you will be an old man like Joseph in our story, surrounded by family and content in a life well-lived. Or perhaps like St. Paul, you might not have physical children but many spiritual children and good works that follow you. Aim to be able to say at the end, "I have kept the faith." That is the ultimate measure of success. All the wealth, achievements, and accolades mean nothing if we abandon our soul. Conversely, even if one's earthly life is humble, holding fast to Christ until the end means a crown of victory (2 Timothy 4:8). To finish well, we must live each day well, and when we don't, repent and course-correct. It's helpful to periodically re-read something inspiring (like this guide, or spiritual classics) to realign yourself. The world's noise can gradually knock us off track; let good inputs pull you back. Stay close to the Eucharist, perhaps as you get older, you can attend daily Mass more frequently since kids may be grown. Keep Our Lady close too; many men consecrate themselves to Jesus through Mary as a way of persevering under her guidance, as she always leads us to her Son. She's a mother who doesn't quit on her children and will pray for you "now and at the hour of our death." And remember, perseverance is ultimately a grace. Yes, it requires our effort, but we persist because God persists with us. He who began a good work in you will bring it to completion (Philippians 1:6). Trust in that. When you feel your strength failing, lean into God's strength. Like the apostles on the stormy sea, cry out "Lord, save me!" and He will grab your hand. Over decades of fidelity, you'll see that it was God's power carrying you far more than your own. Reflection: Do you have brothers in Christ who walk with you? If not, what has prevented you from seeking that fellowship, busyness, fear of vulnerability, not finding the right group? How might you overcome those obstacles? Reflect on times you persevered through a challenge, what helped you then (perhaps a friend's support, a particular scripture, a memory of your purpose)? Conversely, recall if you ever gave up on something important, what might have helped you stick it out? Assess your current spiritual momentum: are you coasting, growing, or stagnating? What would taking it to the "next level" look like for you, and who or what could assist with that? Action Steps:

Connect with Brothers: This week, reach out to an existing men's group or a few friends to initiate fellowship. If your parish has a men's meeting or Knights of Columbus, attend their next gathering just to check it out. If nothing exists, call up two men you respect and propose grabbing breakfast together, mentioning you'd like to share and encourage each other in living the faith. Take the initiative; many men are waiting for an invitation.

Plan a Spiritual Check-up: Schedule at least one "spiritual retreat day" for yourself in the next 6 months. It could be a formal retreat at a retreat house or as simple as a day off work where you go to a quiet place (maybe a monastery or a park), bring a journal and Bible, and reflect on your life with God. Use that time to review your progress, re-evaluate your rule of life, and make any needed adjustments. Treat it like a personal training day for your soul.

[117]

The Fortress Within

Read or Re-read an Inspiring Book: Choose a solid Catholic book or biography of a saint that can fuel your zeal. For example, "The Way" by St. Josemaría Escrivá (a collection of powerful points for daily life) or the life of a saint like St. Augustine, St. Josephine Bakhita, or a modern figure like St. John Paul II. Commit to reading a bit each day. Let their witness renew your motivation to persevere. Maybe even share what you're reading with a friend to spark discussion.

Renew Your Commitments: Take some time to write down the key commitments you've made through this journey (e.g., prayer daily, integrity at work, being present to family, etc.). Create a short "Rule of Life" summary or a list of resolutions. Then consecrate or entrust these commitments to God—perhaps by praying a prayer of surrender or consecration (like offering all these intentions to the Sacred Heart of Jesus or through the Immaculate Heart of Mary). By doing this, you acknowledge that you plan to persevere not by your strength alone but with divine assistance. Keep that written commitment in your Bible or journal to revisit in the future, reminding yourself of the race you are running and the finish line ahead.

Final Exhortation: Build the Fortress

The Fortress Within

The Fortress Within

Brother, you have journeyed through many themes and chapters, each like a stone contributing to the stronghold you are building within. You might feel inspired, or perhaps a bit overwhelmed by all the areas of life touched. Remember this: you don't walk this path alone. God the Father is the architect who has laid out the blueprint of holiness for you. Jesus Christ is the cornerstone of your fortress, without Him, nothing stands. The Holy Spirit is the fire forging you into a man of fortitude. And you are surrounded by the Church, on earth and in heaven, cheering you on. As you set out to implement what you've read, do so with boldness and trust. "Be watchful, stand firm in the faith, act like men, be strong" (1 Corinthians 16:13). "Let all that you do be done in love" (1 Corinthians 16:14). The war is indeed within, but so is the Kingdom of God. Each time you choose prayer over spiritual sloth, honesty over convenience, purity over passion, generosity over greed, courage over fear, you are fortifying that Kingdom – laying another brick in the fortress of virtue. There will be days when the battle is fierce and you might see some stones cracked or sections weak. That's okay. Return to the sacraments; let the Divine Builder restore you. Every Confession rebuilds what sin sought to destroy. Every Eucharist cements you more strongly to Christ, the Rock. Over time, you'll notice changes: sins that used to dominate you lose their grip, habits of goodness become more natural, your family life warms with the light of faith, your perspective on work and money clarifies, and your very presence becomes a source of strength and calm to those around you. This is the fortress shining out. Remember that small keys can open big doors: the small daily fidelities open up immense graces. A short prayer in the morning can redirect a whole day. A tiny act of self-denial can avert a big sin. A single kind word can heal a wounded relationship. Never underestimate the cumulative power of these little acts, like stones upon stones, raising a mighty edifice over the years. Conversely, don't be discouraged by setbacks. Even the strongest walls need maintenance; even the best soldiers need rest and regrouping. What matters is that you keep building, keep guarding, keep advancing. And you are not building just for yourself. Your fortress within shelters those you love. Your wife and children (or those entrusted to your care) find refuge in your strength and love. Your friends and community draw courage from your witness. By being a man of God, you become a bastion for others, like a lighthouse, a sturdy bridge, a safe harbour in the cultural storms. In a world so often devoid of solid anchors, your fidelity can guide others home. What an honour and responsibility that is! But do not fear it, for God has given you all the tools and weapons you need. He believes in you enough to call you to this high standard. And if God is for you, who can be against you? So stand tall. Like Nehemiah rebuilding the walls of Jerusalem, work with one hand and keep your sword of faith ready in the other (cf. Nehemiah 4:17). Protect what is holy. Don't yield an inch to the enemy, if you slip, recover it swiftly. Surround yourself with fellow builders and warriors who will shout words of encouragement when you grow weary. Keep your eyes on Christ; He is on the ramparts with you, and He has already scouted the path to victory. The saints in glory watch and intercede, eager for you to join their ranks when the time comes. A day will dawn when you will lay down your sword and trowel, and the Lord of Hosts will survey the fortress of your soul. By His grace, it will stand not as a monument to your own effort, but as a testimony to what God can do in a man who cooperates with Him. He will see in its stones the likeness of His Son, the true Man of God, and He will welcome you into the eternal stronghold of Heaven. This is the ultimate legacy: to hear the Father say, "Well done, good and faithful servant... Enter into the joy of your master" (Matthew 25:21). Until that day, build the fortress. Fortify it daily with prayer and Sacrament, defend it with virtue and truth, expand it with love and generosity. Make it a place where Christ the King is pleased to dwell. When the winds howl and the arrows fly, you will not be shaken, for your foundation is the Rock of Ages. And from this stronghold, you will march forth to fight the good fight in the world, to protect and provide for those entrusted to you, and to lead souls to the safety of Christ's embrace. Onward, then, Catholic man of God! The war is within, but victory is assured in Jesus. With boldness, wisdom, and the armour of light, go forth and build the fortress within.

Appendix

Rule of Life Template

The Fortress Within

Use this template to craft your personal Rule of Life. Adjust the categories as needed for your state in life. Aim for balance and be realistic. Fill in specific practices or times for each category:

Daily Prayer & Sacraments: (e.g., Morning prayer at ___ AM; Rosary or Scripture reading at ___; Night prayer or Examen at ___; Mass on ___ days; Confession every ___.)

Work & Vocation Duties: (e.g., Work hours from ___ to ___ with focus and integrity; No work emails after ___ PM to protect family time; if a student or retired, substitute primary daily responsibilities.)

Family & Relationships: (e.g., Family dinner at ___; Read to kids at bedtime; Date night with spouse on ___; Call parents on ___; Fellowship with friends on ___.)

Physical Health: (e.g., Wake up at ___; Exercise on ___ [days] at ___; Limit alcohol to ___; In bed by ___ for ___ hours of sleep.)

Digital/Entertainment: (e.g., No phone during prayer or meals; Screen-off curfew at ___ PM; Limit gaming/TV to ___ hours weekly; One tech-free day a week on ___.)

Service & Charity: (e.g., Volunteer at ___ [organization] monthly; Help kids with service project quarterly; Donate ___% income to church/charity; Perform one act of kindness daily.)

The Fortress Within

Weekly Rest & Worship: (e.g., Sunday Mass at ___; Sunday afternoon family activity or rest [no unnecessary work]; Monthly confession on 1st Saturdays; Eucharistic adoration on ___.)

Personal Growth: (e.g., Spiritual reading or study on ___ [days] at ___; Attend men's group on ___; Annual retreat in [month]; Mentor/mentee meeting on ___.)

Use the above as prompts to write out a schedule or set of commitments. Post it where you'll see it. Remember it's a guide, review and adjust it every few months.

Personal Moral Code Worksheet

This worksheet will help you articulate your core moral and spiritual commitments. Reflect and write out responses:

Core Values: List 5 values that are non-negotiable for you (e.g., Honesty, Purity, Charity, Humility, Diligence). For each, write a sentence on what it means in action. ("Honesty, I will speak the truth even when difficult, and not deceive or cheat.")

Key Boundaries: Identify areas of temptation or past weakness and write personal rules to guard against them. ("I will not be alone with the internet late at night" or "I do not drink more than 2 drinks in an evening" or "I avoid gossip at work by excusing myself.")

Family/Friend Commitments: Write down how you intend to treat those close to you. ("I will be faithful to my wife in thought, word, and deed"; "I will be patient and listen to my children"; "I will honour my parents and support them as they age"; "I will stand by my friends in need.")

Work Ethics: Jot down your principles in work/professional life. ("I give an honest day's work; I do not lie on reports; I treat colleagues and subordinates with respect; I will not cut ethical corners for profit.")

Faith Practices: State your commitments to God. ("I keep Sunday holy by attending Mass every week"; "I pray daily"; "I continually seek to grow in understanding the faith"; "I will have no 'gods' (like money or pleasure) before the Lord.")

Review this personal code periodically (perhaps each month or during an annual retreat). You might even share it with a trusted friend or mentor. Use it as a measuring stick for your behaviour – if you slip, confess, recommit, and get back on track. It's like a mission statement for living out your beliefs.

Family Financial Strategy Map

Use this map as a guide to develop a coherent financial plan that aligns with your family's goals and Catholic values:

Family Vision & Goals: Discuss with your spouse (if applicable) what you want your financial future to look like. List goals: e.g., become debt-free by ___; save for a home or education; increase charitable giving; plan for retirement by age ___; reduce work hours to have more family time by ___, etc. Include spiritual goals like "more family time" that financial choices can affect.

Current Financial Snapshot: Write down all sources of income and all expenses (use a monthly budget format). List assets (savings, investments, property) and liabilities (mortgage, loans, credit debt). This is your starting point.

Budget Plan: Create categories for essential expenses (housing, food, utilities, transport, insurance, etc.), then set discretionary categories (dining out, entertainment, etc.), savings, and giving. Ensure total expenses + savings + giving = income (or adjust to make it so). This becomes your monthly budget. If married, both partners should agree on it.

Debt Elimination: If you have debts, outline a strategy (debt snowball or avalanche). Prioritize which debt to tackle first and how much extra you can pay monthly. Mark expected payoff dates. Also plan to avoid new debt (e.g., use cash or debit, freeze credit card use, build an emergency fund to prevent relying on credit).

Savings & Investment: Set specific targets: e.g., "Build emergency fund of 3 months' expenses (~$) by saving $ per month"; "Contribute $___ per month to retirement fund"; "Save $___ over ___ years for children's college." Automate these contributions if possible. Ensure investments (401k, IRA, Pension, etc.) align with Catholic ethics (avoid funds that invest in objectionable Industry, many companies offer faith-based or socially responsible investment options).

Insurance & Will: Check that you have appropriate insurance (health, life, disability, home) to protect your family in emergencies. Make or update a will (and consider a Catholic healthcare proxy and end-of-life directives in line with your faith). Decide if there are charitable causes you want to include. Doing this is an act of stewardship and love for your family to reduce confusion later.

Giving Plan: Decide on a portion of income to give regularly (to church, charities, those in need). Incorporate it into your budget so it's planned, not leftover. Also discuss any larger charitable goals (like funding a scholarship, supporting a missionary, etc.). As your means grow or debts are paid off, aim to increase generosities.

Review Schedule: Set a recurring meeting (monthly or quarterly) with your spouse (or yourself if single) to review the budget and progress on goals. Adjust as needed (for changes in income, new goals, etc.). Also revisit the "vision" annually, goals may evolve as children grow or circumstances change.

By mapping out this strategy, you turn abstract hopes into concrete action steps. It keeps your financial house in order and directed toward not just material wealth, but a true legacy (security for family and resources for God's work). Keep this map accessible (perhaps in a finance binder or digital file) and refer to it whenever making significant financial decisions to ensure they align with your plan.

Recommended Catholic Resources for Men

To continue growing and finding support on your journey, consider these books, programs, and media geared toward Catholic men and living a life of virtue:

Holy Bible (Catholic Edition) – The Word of God is indispensable. A good translation like the Revised Standard Version Catholic Edition (RSV-CE) or New American Bible (NAB), ideally with study notes, can deeply inform your journey.

Catechism of the Catholic Church – The comprehensive guide on what the Church believes and why. Great for reference on any moral or doctrinal question that arises.

"Into the Breach" by Bishop Thomas J. Olmsted – A powerful apostolic exhortation addressed to Catholic Men. It challenges men to heroic virtue and provides practical insights on prayer, family, and evangelization. (Available as a free PDF online and as a video series through the Knights of Columbus.)

"Be a Man!" by Fr. Larry Richards – A straightforward, challenging book where Fr. Larry draws from his experience in men's ministry to call men to live boldly for Christ in all aspects of life.

The Fortress Within

"The Catholic Gentleman" by Sam Guzman – Both a blog/podcast and a book. It offers reflections and practical tips on virtuous manhood, tapping into the wisdom of the saints and a down-to-earth understanding of modern challenges.

"Introduction to the Devout Life" by St. Francis de Sales – A spiritual classic written for laypeople. Though from the 17th century, its advice on prayer, virtue, and facing temptation is timeless and very applicable for a man seeking holiness in the world.

"The Way" (and "Furrow", "Forge") by St. Josemaría Escrivá – Collections of short points/meditations. Easy to read in small bits. These nuggets provoke self-examination and spur you to sanctify everyday life (Escrivá especially speaks to integrating faith into work and daily duties).

"Manual for Men" (Edited by Fr. Richard Heilman) – A compendium of prayers, Church teachings, and writings aimed at Catholic men. It includes the full text of Bishop Olmsted's Into the Breach and many other resources in a handy manual format.

Exodus 90 – A 90-day rigorous spiritual exercise for men that has gained popularity. It involves daily prayer, ascetic practices (like giving up luxuries and many comforts), and fraternity. While challenging, many have found it life-changing in breaking attachments and building discipline.

[130]

Knights of Columbus – Not a book, but joining the K of C can provide fraternity and opportunities for service. They also offer faith formation resources and a network of men dedicated to Church and community.

Men's Conferences/Retreats: (Check your diocese or region) – Attending an annual men's conference can recharge you. Many dioceses hold them, featuring inspiring Catholic speakers. Retreat programs like Christ Renews His Parish (Welcome), Cursillo, or ACTS are specifically aimed at renewing the spiritual life of laymen through community and personal encounter with Christ.

Online Resources & Podcasts: The Catholic Gentleman (blog/podcast), EWTN's The Catholic Café (often addresses men's issues), Matthew Leonard's podcasts or Fr. Mike Schmitz's talks (like on Ascension Presents) often speak to men's hearts in practical ways. These can supplement your reading when you're on the go.

Accountability and Filtering Software: If lust/pornography is an issue, resources like Covenant Eyes or Ever Accountable (internet accountability software) can be useful tools, helping you stick to purity commitments with brotherly accountability.

Parish Life & Ministries: Don't overlook the resources right in your parish: Bible studies, That Man Is You (a structured men's program), Knights of Columbus, volunteer groups (St. Vincent de Paul, etc.). Engaging with these will connect you with like-minded men and keep you grounded in community and service.

Equip yourself with these resources as needed, but remember they are aids to the primary work which is done in prayer, sacraments, and daily life. Pace yourself, you don't have to consume everything at once. Choose what speaks to your current need and dive in. The goal is ongoing growth. As Proverbs says, "He who walks with the wise becomes wise" in a similar way, walking with the wisdom in these books and the fellowship of these groups will help you continue becoming the man God calls you to be. **By God's grace and your perseverance, you will build the fortress within, and in doing so, you'll bless far more lives than just your own.

[134]

Our Father

Our Father, Who art in heaven, hallowed be Thy name; Thy kingdom come; Thy will be done on earth as it is in heaven. Give us this day our daily bread; and forgive us our trespasses as we forgive those who trespass against us; and lead us not into temptation, but deliver us from evil.

Hail Mary

Hail Mary, full of grace. The Lord is with thee. Blessed art thou amongst women, and blessed is the fruit of thy womb, Jesus. Holy Mary, Mother of God, pray for us sinners, now and at the hour of our death, Amen.

The Apostle's Creed

I believe in God, the Father Almighty, Creator of Heaven and earth; and in Jesus Christ, His only Son, Our Lord, Who was conceived by the Holy Ghost, born of the Virgin Mary, suffered under Pontius Pilate, was crucified; died, and was buried. He descended into Hell; the third day He arose again from the dead; He ascended into Heaven, sitteth at the right hand of God, the Father Almighty; from thence He shall come to judge the living and the dead. I believe in the Holy Spirit, the holy Catholic Church, the communion of saints, the forgiveness of sins, the resurrection of the body, and the life everlasting.

The Eternal Father

Eternal Father, I offer you the Body and Blood, Soul and Divinity of Your Dearly Beloved Son, Our Lord, Jesus Christ, in atonement for our sins and those of the whole world.

On the Ten Small Beads of Each Decade

For the sake of His sorrowful Passion, have mercy on us and on the whole world.

Repeat for the remaining decades

Saying the "Eternal Father" (6) on the "Our Father" bead and then 10 "For the sake of His sorrowful Passion" (7) on the following "Hail Mary" beads.

Conclude with Holy God (Repeat three times)

Holy God, Holy Mighty One, Holy Immortal One, have mercy on us and on the whole world.

Optional Closing Prayer

Eternal God, in whom mercy is endless and the treasury of compassion--inexhaustible, look kindly upon us and increase Your mercy in us, that in difficult moments we might not despair nor become despondent, but with great confidence submit ourselves to Your holy will, which is Love and Mercy itself.

The Fortress Within

Notes

The Fortress Within

Notes

The Fortress Within

Notes

The Fortress Within

Notes

Printed by Amazon Italia Logistica S.r.l.
Torrazza Piemonte (TO), Italy